D0268686

FIT TO BUST

A COMIC TREASURE CHEST

"What do you get when you combine musical talent with lactation? Fit to Bust – a gloriously joyful celebration of the breastfeeding life. This is truly a unique contribution to lactation literature, which will be enjoyed by the whole family."

Veronika Robinson, Editor, *The Mother* magazine

"Humanicum breastfeedicus is a fairly common species and has a great sense of humour."

Deborah Jackson, author of *Three in a Bed* and *Baby Wisdom*

Published by Lonely Scribe
www.lonelyscribe.co.uk

ISBN: 978-1-905179-10-7

FIT TO BUST

A COMIC TREASURE CHEST

Compiled by Alison Blenkinsop
in support of Baby Milk Action

Lonely Scribe

Contents

Acknowledgements

Countless people have helped and encouraged me during the creation of this book. These are at the top of my list:

My family

My husband Tony gives me unconditional love and affection, and makes me laugh every day. My late mother, Stella Fookes, nourished me with her milk and helped me develop all my talents. My father, Tom Fookes, gave me a portion of his skills in music and parody, and still encourages me. Their daily prayers and loving support have enabled me to grow spiritually as well as physically and mentally. My sisters Mary Fookes, Elizabeth Payne (formerly Ricketts) and Shirley Pearce inspire me with their ideas, laugh obediently when I ring them at midnight with the latest song, and make helpful suggestions.

Colleagues

Lactation Consultants of Great Britain (LCGB) gave me opportunities to sing at meetings and conferences, and develop various teaching resources. Many other breastfeeding specialists helped in writing and promoting the first edition of this book.

Friends and acquaintances

Special thanks go to Judith Bradley, Tania Lappin and Polly Strong and their husbands and children, who taught me the joys and challenges of breastfeeding beyond babyhood. I am very grateful for all I have learned from the many mothers, fathers and babies I've encountered over the years, and for their generous sharing of photographs and stories.

Patti Rundall and Baby Milk Action

This organisation, under its inspirational director Patti Rundall OBE, works tirelessly in highlighting the need to curb the promotion of breastmilk substitutes around the world. Book sales will help them continue this challenging task.

The contacts section at the end of the book gives information about many groups and organisations which encourage and facilitate a natural approach to infant feeding.

Preface

Fit to Bust is a light-hearted, personal look at breastfeeding and related subjects for both general and specialist readership. Part Two looks more closely at various important issues, and includes educational and promotional activities for voluntary and professional supporters. I have no wish to judge or condemn those unable or unwilling to breastfeed, as I am well aware of the challenges posed by cultural opposition and physical difficulties. I hope that this book will go some way to help with their removal!

Permission is given for my own songs and poetry to be used in social events and study days, provided that my name and website details are always given with them. I take no responsibility for obtaining official permission (where needed) for any public performances given by others. In songs referring to male infants, feminine pronouns can be substituted in most places.

Some information, for example on voluntary support groups, pertains largely to the UK, but may well apply to other western countries. Wherever possible, I have checked facts and given credit where it is due. If any omission or error is found, amendments will be made in future editions, as they have been in this second edition.

Abbreviations

For ease of reading, the following are used:

BF   breastfeeding

BN   biological nurturing

BFC   voluntary breastfeeding counsellor or supporter, with accredited training by a national organisation

GP   general practitioner (family or community doctor)

HV   health visitor

KMC   kangaroo mother care

LCGB Lactation Consultants of Great Britain

LC   current or former IBCLC (International Board
            Certified Lactation Consultant)*

MW   midwife

NHS   National Health Service (UK)

Unicef United Nations Children's Fund

WHO   World Health Organisation

NB: The words 'formula' and 'babymilk' describe any artificially manu-
factured breastmilk substitute, as these terms are in common usage.
'Bottle-feeding' may refer to the giving of human or substitute milk.

---

* I have chosen this comprehensive title to acknowledge the achievements of
those who can no longer use the title IBCLC.

Preface to second edition

Since the book's first appearance in 2008, it has been read around the world, including in North America, Europe, the Gulf, Africa, the Indian subcontinent, China and the Antipodes. Coincidentally, it came out at the same time as several other light-hearted breastfeeding books in the UK. Favourable reviews are given on Amazon bookstore's American and UK websites, and many parenting sites, through which it can also be ordered. *Fit to Bust* has its own Facebook page. This new edition has been extensively revised to update and reorder the information, with a separate section for readers wanting more detail, though I hope the first part will leave all readers wanting more!

Pen Press and Lonely Scribe

Pen Press, an independent company, published the first edition of this book in 2008. I am very grateful for their patience with my many amendments, and for the attractive volume they produced.

I am delighted that Lonely Scribe has taken over publication to bring the book to a wider reader-ship. Many thanks to publishing director Susan Last and her team

Helping Tania and baby Anna

for their encouragement and support. It seems especially fitting that during the preparation of this new edition, Susan gave birth at home to her third breastfed baby, Ada, and trained as a breastfeeding supporter, while managing director Tom Cairns and his wife Aby welcomed their fifth baby, Felix, into the family. He too is thriving on mum's milk.

Introduction

Music and word games have always been important in our family, and like Jane Austen's Elizabeth Bennet, we dearly love a laugh. I started piano lessons at the age of six, and developed a talent for accompanying in my teens. I began writing verse and song parodies in senior school. One of my form-mates, Pat Duran (née Tanner), donated a silver cup to the school as a music award, and I was the first winner. In a review of this book on Amazon.com, she recalls a concert in which I sang 'Tit Willow' from *The Mikado*, and says it must surely have been a sign of things to come!

I have amassed a large collection of personalised songs for family, friends and colleagues, verses written for parties and holidays, poems of faith, and hymns. These include a few rhymes in French and Urdu, and some worship songs translated into English from Pakistani languages. My three sisters also write songs; Mary composes music too, writing many songs for junior school assemblies and plays. The family enjoys making music together, surprising unwary guests at mealtimes by singing grace in four parts. Tony has dubbed us the 'Shut Your Trap Family Singers'.

This interest in verse and song-writing is inherited from our nonagenarian father, who composed this poem at the age of 82. (For my own Jerusalem-inspired song, see the Postscript.)

Farewell Jerusalem (sorry, Blake)

They brought him his bow of burning gold,
but he found it much too hot to hold;
the arrows burnt his fingers so
he had to let the darned things go.

They brought him his chariot of fire,
but it had a leak in the offside tyre;
the clouds refused to disappear,
and he found he couldn't lift his spear.

That left the sword and the mental fight,
but the foe appealed against the light,
so he left off building Jerusalem
and ended up in Croydon Crem.

Tom Fookes, 27 September 2001

I've been writing songs about childbirth and feeding for ten years. My father listens with interest, unless we're having lunch, when heavy sighs indicate that the only part he is interested in right now is 'refrain'.

Midwifery and lactation consultancy

I started my nursing training in 1969 at Guy's Hospital, and continued with midwifery at King's College Hospital, both in London. I then spent thirteen years in Pakistan as a partner with the Church Mission Society, returning in 1990 with chronic fatigue syndrome (ME). My recovery was slow, until I discovered that lying in cold water at 16°C for twenty minutes every morning increased my energy, and cleared my stuffy head. On returning to midwifery practice at St George's Hospital in South London two years later, I was delighted to renew acquaintance with my former midwifery tutor. Dora Henschel MBE had been instrumental in setting up the UK Joint Breastfeeding Initiative in the early 1990s. She reawakened my interest in breast-feeding, and I found a new direction to my work.

In 1994 I married Tony (who was well worth the long wait) and we set up home in south-west London. One day my neighbour Christine invited me for a meal, and I felt quite at home when three-year-old William took advantage of her lap to help himself to a liquid lunch. Such behaviour is normal in Pakistan, if not (yet) in English suburbia.

INTRODUCTION

Many of the mothers and babies in the local maternity unit seemed to find breastfeeding a challenge, and I longed to help them more effectively. I couldn't train with a voluntary organisation, as they all require personal experience, so I embarked on studies to qualify as a lactation consultant (IBCLC).* This involved learning about breast-feeding over the first two years of infancy. Fortunately, I could draw on the experience of my friends Judith and Tania, who were both nursing toddlers during this time.

In 1998, I spent a month on the Breastfeeding: Practice and Policy course at the Institute of Child Health in London, together with participants from all parts of the globe. That enthralling course gave me enough confidence to pass the LC exam in 1999. The same year, I won The British Hospital for Mothers and Babies Award for Practice in Support of Breastfeeding for my educational and promotional work. The next year I was awarded a Diploma of Higher Education in Midwifery Studies. In 2001, I took on the role of Infant Feeding Adviser in a shared post at another Surrey hospital, and moved house to Aldershot in north-east Hampshire. At the same time, I became secretary of Lactation Consultants of Great Britain. Both posts taught me a great deal about all aspects of breastfeeding, and gave much inspiration for songs and other celebrations of parenthood.

Drying up

I took early retirement from the NHS at the end of 2006, but continued with my private lactation consultancy 'enABle' (enjoy nursing! Alison Blenkinsop – lactation empowerment). I decided not to renew my LC certification at the end of 2009, and private work is now drying up. I've also stopped writing for professional journals and books and speaking at childbirth conferences. (My presentations usually ended with a relevant song for all to join in!) The finale comes

---

* For more information about becoming a Lactation Consultant, see the LCGB website at www.lcgb.org.

on my sixtieth birthday in March 2011, when I plan to stage a local theatre show entitled *The Mammary Dialogues*, based on interviews with breastfeeding friends and entertainments of various kinds.

My musical activities continue, as I'm a piano accompanist for musicians and choral groups. That part of my work is called 'HOPE' – (Helping Others Perform Enjoyably) – which could also describe my enABle work. In 1997 I trained as a pastoral assistant (PA) with the Diocese of Guildford, and now have a Certificate in Ministry Studies. I'm on the pastoral and music teams at St Michael's Church in Aldershot, playing both organ and my grand piano 'Mahogany', which currently lives at St Michael's. The PA's role involves prayerful listening. Midwives and piano accompanists too need to listen carefully, and to know when to act, and when to sit back.

I hope that you too can now sit back and enjoy this celebration of parenthood and breastfeeding. Who knows? One day the text-speak term ROFL (roll on floor laughing) may be replaced by LFTB (laugh fit to bust)!

Rule, breastfeeding!
(tune: 'Rule, Britannia!')

For many years I have been writing humorous songs,
to raise awareness of the many things that steal breastfeeding's
*   heart and soul;*
and now I have a book to enable me to reach that goal.
This is my purpose, to help correct those wrongs,
and raise funds for Baby Milk Action's vital role.

Love, and Mum's milk, will save the world, I trust;
learn all about it while you're laughing fit to bust!

INTRODUCTION

Can't stop feedin' that child
(tune: 'Can't help lovin' dat man'
from *Showboat*)

*O hear me pleadin', I love
my feedin' time,
I don't have to say why –
there's every reason why
I should nurse my child;
on my decision all the
angels have smiled.*

*Mums should be happy,
babies should thrive,
I'm gonna feed my child
till he's five;
can't stop feedin' that babe
of mine.
Maybe he's greedy, maybe
he's vile,
maybe he's just a lactophile;
can't stop feedin' that babe of
mine.*

Still breastfeeding? Goodness!

*When he's by my heart streams of nectar start,
and when he's replete, he then beguiles with joyful smiles.
Tell me I'm selfish, tell me I'm mean,
give me a hundred reasons to wean,
can't stop feedin' that babe of mine!*

Forewords

Patti Rundall OBE, Policy Director, Baby Milk Action
www.babymilkaction.org

This book been produced by a long-time supporter to help Baby Milk Action protect breastfeeding and end the irresponsible marketing of breastmilk substitutes, which puts so many children's lives at risk. In areas with unsafe water a bottle-fed child is up to twenty-five times more likely to die as a result of diarrhoea. Reversing the decline in breastfeeding could save 1.5 million lives around the world every year.

Baby Milk Action is a non-profit organisation that works within the International Baby Food Action Network, IBFAN. The book's production is entirely independent of Baby Milk Action, and the organisation takes no responsibility for any of its contents.

Heather Welford, writer and NCT breastfeeding counsellor and tutor
www.heatherwelford.co.uk

Another book about breastfeeding? Yes – but this one really is different. Alison has not written it as a 'how to' book, though there is plenty of information in it which will help a mother wanting to find out more about the topic of breastfeeding. More importantly, it will give her confidence, plus a sense of friendship and warmth. Alison's knowledge of breastfeeding is rooted in her understanding of it not just as a process of transferring the milk the baby needs, but as part of a deeply wonderful and joyful relationship. She does all this with humour – sometimes to produce a smile, sometimes a wry nod of agreement, sometimes a giggle and sometimes a laugh-out-loud chortle.

Alison loves words, music and the properties they share to teach us, entertain us and bring us together. *Fit to Bust* brings her unique talents to an audience made up of anyone and everyone – but it will be especially welcome to parents who have known the love that comes from nurturing a child, and to all the understanding carers, friends and professionals who share Alison's commitment to supporting them.

Jasmine Birtles, finance journalist, author and comedian
www.moneymagpie.com

Whether you're trying to breastfeed, wanting to help others or just interested in the subject, Alison's book is a cornucopia of fascinating breastfeeding facts, jokes, poems, cartoons and ideas. Who says you have to be po-faced to promote the benefits of feeding your baby in a natural way? Alison has certainly seen the funny side as well as the serious facts.

As someone who has never had a baby and never breastfed, I am, of course, a world expert on breastfeeding. In fact, I have spoken at two major breastfeeding conferences, which I think is pretty impressive for someone who has never produced milk in her life. It's certainly something I like to boast about at dinner-parties. It was at one of these conferences that I met Alison and we got on immediately.

I was introduced to the whole concept of breastfeeding through my mother, who runs a doula agency. Supporting breastfeeding is one of the tasks of doulas and it was talking to them that made me realise how something so natural has become so unnecessarily difficult and controversial in our society. Of course, some mothers physically can't produce milk and many have strong personal reasons why they don't want to, but there are many others who have no idea of the benefits and just go straight to the bottle because their friends are doing it or because they failed at the first attempt.

Mothers in Britain need more gentle, fun and helpful encouragement to breastfeed – in the way that Alison writes in this book. There are so many benefits – long-term health of mother and baby, emotional bonding and it is even a natural contraceptive I am told. As a financial journalist I also always point out the cash advantage of breast rather than the bottle. Just by breastfeeding for the first six months, new mothers can save upwards of £500. As raising children becomes more expensive in this country, every bit of saving really counts. So, enjoy Alison's book and help spread the word!

PART ONE

An everyday affair: The normality of breastfeeding

Chapter 1

A precious resource

An overview of the value of human milk

Breastfeeding ensured our survival as *Homo Sapiens* (which is an anagram of OO, ME HAS NIPS), babies being *Homo Sucky-ends*. There's plenty of evidence that mammalian feeding ensures bonding and infant safety, as well as nutrition. The University of Notre Dame in the US reported in 2010 that child-rearing practices common in hunter-gatherer societies are associated with better mental health, greater empathy and higher intelligence, compared with the 'civilised' way of raising children today.

This song celebrates those ancient practices, thought to be part of every human's experience for about ninety-nine percent of our history. The modern version of such behaviour has become known in industrialised societies as 'attachment parenting' and is the subject of Jean Liedloff's book *The Continuum Concept*. In developing countries, it is so common that it has no name.

Help yourself!

FIT TO BUST

The good old days
(tune: 'Clementine')

Refrain
*Feeding babies, feeding babies needn't be a mystery,
let's recall how we developed in our human history.*

Once our homeland was the jungle;
we commuted through the trees,
clasping babes to hairy bosoms -
frequent feeding was a breeze.
We possessed no clocks or bottles,
milk was never pumped and stored;
and our young, like little limpets,
used our chests as bed and board.

Refrain

We relied on other mothers
if our milk supply should fail,
and the tongue-ties were divided
with a sharpened finger-nail.
Day and night we kept together
(many risks our children faced);
long lactation gave contraception,
so our young were widely spaced.

Refrain

Stone Age meals were fruit and veggies,
and perhaps a roasted beast;
given pre-chewed little pieces,
babes enjoyed a mammoth feast.
With no jars of turkey purée,
how our children were deprived!
It is really quite amazing
that the human race survived.

1. A PRECIOUS RESOURCE

Last refrain
Feeding babies, feeding babies
easily and healthily
just requires a little knowledge
of our human history.

For another song on the same theme, written for a Women's Institute meeting and based on 'Jerusalem', see the Postscript.

It's tempting to imagine a golden age when all mothers breastfed with no difficulty. Statues of heavy-breasted goddesses show that many ancient societies held lactating women in high regard. But there is evidence dating from the third century BC that artificial feeding with human or animal milk has always been used as well. LC Carolyn Westcott has a fascinating collection of equipment used in Europe during the last two centuries, including nipple shields, breast relievers, 'sucking glasses' to remove milk, and feeding bottles. Similar items are shown in *The History of the Feeding Bottle*.*

Fine Domestic Product

When mother's own milk wasn't available, wet-nursing by another woman provided a tasty solution for thousands of years, and is still normal in some countries. But in today's western society, partly due to decades of advertisements for commercial baby foods, the importance and value of human milk is largely unrecognised. Though one of the world's most precious natural resources, it is never mentioned in statistics of a country's GDP (Gross Domestic Product); yet to replace it totally would cost a fortune.

I have never yet found a reference to breastfeeding on TV or radio programmes dedicated to food, nor in most advice on healthy eating for children. Any mention of breastmilk, even in NHS England's Start4Life campaign, seems limited to babies under one year. A similar gap is noticeable in many medical diagrams of the female

---

* www.babybottle-museum.co.uk

body. Breasts are often omitted, or linked in some vague way to the reproductive organs (as an invitation to sexual activity, perhaps?). Using them for feeding offspring is often viewed as a lifestyle choice, rather than an integral part of childbearing and mothering.

Green milk

Growing environmental concerns have led to a calculation of how far our food travels before it arrives on our plate, and how much carbon is used to put it there; the lower the figure, the 'greener' the food. Gabrielle Palmer, author of The Politics of Breastfeeding, points out that breastmilk has the smallest carbon footprint of any food, and zero food miles.[1]

Professional ignorance

The education of paediatricians, GPs and dietitians does not include mandatory teaching from an infant feeding specialist, and many rely on babyfood companies for advice on nutrition. During their year's course, health visitors may receive only half a day's training on the subject. This may even be given by a formula company representative, or more accurately, salesperson. Trainee midwives do receive more education than this, but because they work alongside registered midwives who qualified some years earlier, outdated knowledge is often recycled. Moreover, few maternity units provide mandatory updates to ensure that practice remains evidence-based. Many health workers see nothing inappropriate in attending study days funded by a babymilk company, and then advertising its wares by using branded stationery items. (See Chapter 21)

Poor breastfeeding support is endemic in Britain. Although health workers are personally accountable for the care they give, the responsibility for adequate training rests with the National Health Service. But everyone needs to understand infant feeding, not just health workers. Perhaps we can learn from animal role models.

1. A PRECIOUS RESOURCE

Let's nurse our young
(tune: 'Let's do it, let's fall in love' by Cole Porter)

Cats do it, rats do it,
topsy-turvy vampire bats do it,
let's do it, let's nurse our young.
Cows do it, sows do it,
monkeys swinging through the boughs do it,
let's do it, let's nurse our young.

Mares do it, hares do it,
chilled-out furry polar bears do it,
let's do it, let's nurse our young.
Goats do it, stoats do it,
tigers wearing stripy coats do it,

let's do it, let's nurse our young.

Skunks do it, chipmunks do it,
jumbos with corrugated trunks do it,
let's do it, let's nurse our young.
Moles do it, voles do it,
wily weasels in their holes do it,
let's do it, let's nurse our young.

Dogs do it, wart-hogs do it,
beavers beavering with logs do it,
let's do it, let's nurse our young.
Shrews do it, gnus do it,
tabby cats in London mews do it,
let's do it, let's nurse our young!

For a closer look at how animals nurture their young, see Chapter 20.

The sophistication and technology of western life has distanced us from our roots. Few people realise that a lack of extended breast-feeding plays a part in the increasing prevalence of many infant and adult conditions like glue ear, tooth decay and dental malocclusion, cow's milk allergy and obesity. This is because formula promotion was well under way in 1951, as my birth weight card (opposite) shows.[*]

Fortunately, my mother didn't want me to be *beast* fed, so my rapid weight gain was entirely natural.

I sent a copy of the next song to Sir Cliff Richard, and received a message from his personal assistant that he didn't think he'd ever sing it, much as he'd enjoyed it. Thanks, Cliff!

Lactation sensation
(tune: 'Congratulations')

Human lactation is a sensation;
it gives the purest food to babies from their birth.

---

[*] I'm not sure our Royal Family are a good advertisement for this company!

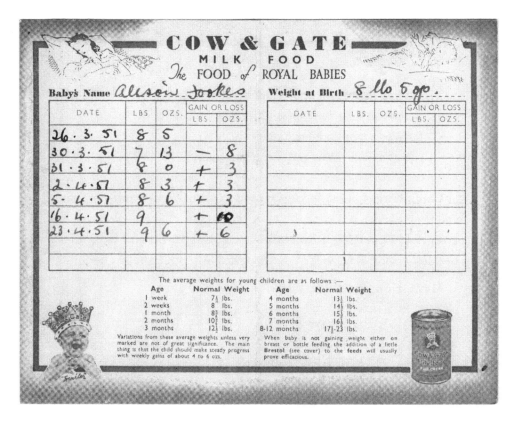

Its application by every nation
would maximise the health of everyone on earth.

So we should all encourage its initiation;
colostrum is the baby's first inoculation,
and early feeds increase affection in the mother
so to each other attachment is made.

Human lactation has a relation
to lowered rates of illness and of allergy;
this milk's ingestion improves digestion,
providing healthy protein, fat and energy.

And mothers' milk gives infants more than good nutrition;
the suckling helps establish optimal dentition,

and also hinders the return of ovulation
so procreation is safely delayed!

Human lactation's appreciation
is sadly lacking in some areas today,
but dedication to education
will raise this battle cry: "Lactation rules, OK!"

Confidence in breastfeeding is hard to maintain in the face of apathy, and even harder if it is positively discouraged. My nephew Peter was born in 1972 in Perth Royal Infirmary, after an arduous labour. In the evening, a midwife brought the drug trolley to Elizabeth's bed.

MW: Here are your tablets.

E: What are they?

MW: Don't worry, everyone has them.

E: I can't take anything without knowing what it's for!

MW: This one's to dry up your milk, and that's a sleeping pill.

Elizabeth declined to take either because she was determined to breastfeed – along with only one other in a ward of sixteen mothers! The situation has now greatly improved because of Scotland's sustained work in BF promotion over the last decade.

Food for thought

Breastfeeding is known to be important for optimal brain development. Yet a 2008 *Daily Telegraph* report stated that the UK had one of the lowest breastfeeding rates in Europe. It was also ranked lowest in a Unicef study in 2007 examining child well-being in rich countries.[2] These two factors are linked.

1. A PRECIOUS RESOURCE

The British Government's Department of Health produces a five-yearly report on infant feeding. The 2005 survey shows that around seventy-six percent of UK babies start on the breast. By six months, only one in four is getting any human milk, with a negligible number breast-feeding exclusively in line with DH recommendations.[3] Compare this with Norway, where all newborns start on mother's milk, and eighty percent are taking nothing else at six months. But this is made possible by strict controls on formula promotion, and a year's maternity leave as standard. So we know what would help the UK!

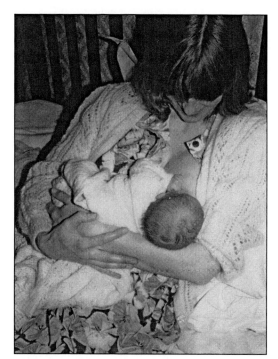

First immunisation No sharp points needed

Glorious food!
(tune: 'Food, glorious food' from *Oliver!*)

Milk, glorious food, first
juvenile diet;
what should it include for babies to buy it?
Cream, sweetness and growing power,
this answers the question,
incessantly flowing for
quick digestion!

33

Milk, wonderful food, all babies require it;
when it's from the boob, all babies desire it.
It's freely available,
needs no preparation,
warm, healthy and flavourful,
pure sensation!

Milk made by our mums brings health to the nation,
and fills little tums with blissful elation.
There's no real alternative,
life-giving and free;
it's great – let's highly rate and celebrate
this glorious food!

Found in an online search: 'Colostrum is probably the best and most complete single supplement for supporting the immune system.' Supplement? Ah yes, produced by a cow or sheep, then put into capsules and sold at vast expense by the 'health' industry as a cure for all kinds of adult disorders – which might not have arisen had the human version been given years earlier.

How are we doing in the UK?

The Department of Health's spending on breastfeeding promotion, per baby, is a tiny proportion of formula companies' outlay on advertising.[4] Moreover, their promotional campaigns don't always give the right message.

On postcards sent to maternity staff for distribution during Breastfeeding Awareness Week in 2004, the first statement read: 'Day One: your baby probably won't be interested in feeding.' I wonder what message that would give the average first-time mother? My card went in the bin!

1. A PRECIOUS RESOURCE

The next year, one of three BAW posters showed a father holding a baby. He is extolling the virtues of giving expressed breastmilk, which lets his partner rest while he has some special time with Jack. Many of us left that poster off the wall or covered up the text. However, its display elsewhere led to an increase in calls to breastfeeding counsellor (BFC) helplines, for information on expressing and giving bottles to very young babies.

Promotional materials in other years were inspired. One set of stunning black-and-white photographs of families from a wide range of backgrounds won a national award for diversity.

The NHS's budget for breastfeeding support is a victim of cost savings, despite the fact that increasing the incidence of BF would greatly reduce future outlay on health treatments. Recent boosts to funding have not been maintained, so resources are still very limited. At the time of writing, some maternity units are employing Breastfeeding Support Workers on Band 2.[*] In some cases, there is no requirement for any credentials beyond enthusiasm and an unqualified 'knowledge of infant feeding', with no referral route to a BF specialist. See BFC Charlotte Thomas's blogs on the website www.iwantmymum.com for more information.

A plug for breastfeeding support

The NHS also relies on unpaid helpers to plug the gaps. The four national voluntary organisations have developed excellent training courses for volunteers with personal BF experience. Their qualifications enable them to listen to and support new parents, referring them to specialist lactation management and medical advice where appropriate. (Breastfeeding counsellors have comprehensive theoretical and practical training over many months; peer supporters are educated in shorter programmes to give general encouragement.) They often encounter problems caused by negligence and ignorance

---

[*] Information on NHS pay scales is available online.

in the health service. LC Sharon Breward MBE, with tongue very firmly in cheek, commented in the LCGB newsletter *Treasure Chest* in 2004:

> *Imagine going into hospital with a broken leg and being*
> *told that there is no specialist to treat you, but being given*
> *the phone number of someone who broke their leg last*
> *year in order to sort it out!*

However, it's important to encourage a less health-orientated view of breastfeeding – it isn't a medical condition, but a social interaction! Hospital-based BF clinics provide help for feeding problems, but community drop-in groups can also offer general encouragement in a more homely atmosphere. One example of such provision is The Baby Café ®, which was born in 2005 with NHS funding. There are now Baby Cafés in many parts of the country.

'Making breastfeeding fashionable' is the slogan of Little Angels, a Community Interest Company started by mothers in Lancashire to offer peer support in areas where bottle-feeding had become culturally embedded. The Be A Star campaign, set up in March 2008, took this further to show that breastfeeding could be glamorous too. Full-size posters at bus stops displayed local young women posing like fashion models, with a baby at the breast. Advertisements across Lancashire, and on local radio stations and the internet, explained that these women aren't celebrities, but stars! (See Chapter 17 for more information on breastfeeding supporters.)

Best Beginnings

Real improvements in UK breastfeeding promotion are now being made from other non-NHS funded groups. In the forefront is Alison Baum,[*] winner of the Sheila McKechnie Award in 2007 for her Health and Social Care campaigns. Alison, a former producer and director of science documentaries at the BBC, is the mother of two children,

---

[*] Alison is pictured at the end of Chapter 9.

Abingdon Baby Café's 'Don't Bring a Bottle' party

both breastfed in very challenging circumstances. She established the charity Best Beginnings in 2006 to end child health inequalities, starting with a focus on infant feeding.

So far, the charity has founded the Breastfeeding Manifesto Coalition,* and created an art exhibition entitled Get Britain Breastfeeding. With funding from the Department of Health, it has produced the multi-lingual DVD *From Bump to Breastfeeding*. This film uses real-life stories as well as specialist guidance, and is intended for free distribution to the 600,000 women who embark on pregnancy each year. It can be also viewed on the Best Beginnings website. Another DVD on caring for premature babies, *Small Wonders*, is due for release in 2011.

** See the end of chapter 22.

Global celebration

In May 2006, the Philippines broke the Guinness World Record for Simultaneous Breastfeeding in a Single Site when they gathered 3,738 women within the City of Manila. The oldest nursing mother there was 51-year-old Rosanna Robles.

World Breastfeeding Week is celebrated annually at the start of August. Its organisers, the World Alliance for Breastfeeding Action (WABA), choose a topic each year. In 2008, it was related to the forthcoming Olympic Games with the slogan 'Mother Support: Going for the Gold'. The theme for 2009 was breastfeeding as a vital response in emergency situations, and in 2010 the focus was on the Baby Friendly Ten Steps to Successful Breastfeeding.[*]

Whichever way you look at it, breastfeeding is here to stay.

> Breastfeeding is a beautiful, peaceful and powerful experience. It is giving your baby the perfect food in the perfect way. You don't have to be perfect to do something that is perfect. How many chances in life do you have to do that?
>
> Dia Michels[5]

> A pair of substantial mammary glands have the advantage over the two hemispheres of the most learned professor's brain in the art of compounding a nutritive fluid for infants.
>
> Oliver Wendell Holmes, Chief Justice (1809–94)

---

[*] See chapter 17 for more information on the Ten Steps.

Chapter 2
Oh what a lovely pair

Support for the noble bosom

I was thrilled when my breasts appeared. In the 1960s, circle-stitched bras were in fashion, but I had to sharpen my shape with hankies tucked inside less exotic underwear. Breasts themselves were rather hidden away and rarely mentioned in public, but over recent years they've become the subject of much discussion, along with their containers.

Over-shoulder boulder holders and more elevated attire

A 1993 TV documentary entitled 'Giving the Empire a Lift' featured the Knightsbridge lingerie store of Rigby and Peller, corsetières to the Queen. A saleswoman was shown helping a well-endowed client to find the right size. As one of the bras struggled to accommodate its double load, she remarked, "That's no good, we can't have them talking to each other, can we?"

In the BBC Radio 4 programme 'Ayres on the Air' in 2004, Pam Ayres was talking about buying a new uplift bra. It was very pretty but impractical, as whenever she bent down to feed the cat, all the goods fell off the shelf. But the experience inspired her to write this poem:

The Wonderbra

I bought myself a Wonderbra
*   for fourteen ninety-nine.*
It looked so good on the model girl's chest,
*   and I hoped it would on mine.*

I took it from the packaging
  and when I tried it on,
the Wonderbra restored to me
  all I believed had gone.
It gave me such a figure,
  I can't believe it's mine,
I showed it to my husband
  and it made his eyeballs shine.
And when I served the breakfast,
  the kids cried out, "Hooray!
Here comes our darling mother,
  with her bosom on a tray!'"
I didn't really need one,
  my present bra, it's true,
had only been in constant use
  since nineteen eighty-two.
But the silhouette I dreamed about
  is mine, is mine at last,
and builders on the scaffolding
  drop off as I walk past.[6]

Bamboobzled

Many women complain that they can never find a good fit, but the range of styles available is mind-boggling. They can buy a 'balcony' bra, which I suppose is appropriate for anything connected with Upper Circles. There are also full-cup, half-cup, soft-cup, multi-way, halter-neck, shock-absorber (useful for public feeding?), underwired, T-shirt, sports, push-up, plunge, strapless, shelf, and even rhinestone-studded bras. And ones for nursing, of course: drop-cup, zip, sleep and 'express yourself' bras, made of cotton, polyester, microfibre and also bamboo!
  And that's not all:

2. OH WHAT A LOVELY PAIR

The Civil Service bra makes mountains out of molehills
The Communist bra suppresses the masses
The Salvation Army bra uplifts the fallen
The Presbyterian bra makes them firm and upright
The Sheepdog bra rounds them up and points them in the right direction[7]

Sizing up the situation

Have you ever wondered why the letters A to H are used to grade bra sizes? I found this explanation on the internet:

A   Almost Boobs

B   Barely there

C   Can't Complain

D   Dang!

DD   Double dang!

E   Enormous

F   Fake

G   Get a Reduction

H   Help me, I've fallen and can't get up!

This is not just, M&S

In 2009, pressure from a group called Busts4Justice forced the company Marks and Spencer to remove their £2 surcharge on bras larger than a DD cup. M&S turnover was boosted by their contrite "We've boobed" response. The story has been immortalised in a portrait by world-famous photographer Uli Weber. It shows the executive chairman dangling a generous brassière, with the marketing director clutching a pair of melons.

Bras for special needs

A bra that converts into two gas masks, for both the wearer and a needy bystander, won an Ig Nobel Prize for Public Health in 2009. The designer, Elena Bodnor, can be seen in a video posted on YouTube by Improbable Research, whose aim is 'to make people laugh then think'. Dr Bodnor is shown delving into her clothes to remove a scarlet underwired brassière, then separating it into two parts to cover the faces of real Nobel Prize winners.

Goats in Pakistan are often seen clad in bras, but not for uplift. The udder is covered with a bag to limit kids' suckling, so the owner can sell the milk.

The Daily Telegraph newspaper chose a new use for old bras as one of its Pictures of the Day for 9 September 2010. Swindon farmer Rowie Meers discovered the perfect support for her drooping Galia melons 'right under her nose'. However, her cup size wasn't large enough, so helpful customers sent her dozens of their own DD cast-offs. She was grateful for their support, and hoped to acquire even larger bras when the farm started growing watermelons.

Flash bulbs
A young man was training as a waiter in a posh restaurant in London. When a woman diner helped herself from the dish he was holding, a breast fell out of her low-cut dress. To spare her blushes, the waiter swiftly replaced it with another serving spoon. Calling him over, the head waiter murmured, "Well done, lad, but remember that at the Ritz, we always warm the spoon first."

Western men's interest in breasts can lead to trouble. *The Daily Telegraph* reported a story in the summer of 2010 about two young women in Paris who displayed their breasts to a man as he used a cash machine, then fled with his money. The French police warned people not to be distracted as they used ATMs, "however attractive the view".

Others may not admire the view. In his book *Babes and Sucklings*, Nigel Rees quotes the story of a five-year-old's refusal to wear a V-neck sweater. His mother was puzzled until he explained: "I don't want one like that. My teacher has one and when she bends down, you can see her lungs."[8]

Selling points

In the second half of the twentieth century, advertisers began to use breasts to sell all sorts of merchandise. The British starlet and pin-up Sabrina, who had a 17-inch waist and 42½-inch bust, was refreshingly upfront about her lack of talent; her entire career was built on her bosom. She used her assets to great effect in the 1950s and '60s in promotions for such diverse goods as Caltex motor grease, caravans and nylon stockings. In one ad, she's pointing out that a certain brand of photographic gear provides 'The World's Finest Projection Equipment'. Today's commercials are much more subtle, but many still make use of the Sabrina effect.[9]

With such an emphasis on breast appearance rather than function, it is no surprise that many women fear that breastfeeding will ruin their figure. But any sagging comes from pregnancy, advancing years and genetics rather than feeding. The model Nell McAndrew showed no signs of losing her figure in photo-shoots taken while she was breastfeeding.[10]

Some women stay pert all their life; others are less fortunate. Harking back nostalgically to newly-wed life, the comedian Joan Rivers complained that whenever she removed her bra in later years, her husband would shout 'TIMBER!'

Valerie Finigan's amusing book *Saggy Boobs and Other Breastfeeding Myths* is a great confidence-booster for new mothers.

Fears of having the wrong shape or size of breast for successful feeding are unfounded, as the next song explains.

Size doesn't matter!
(tune: 'Sailor's Hornpipe')

Do your boobs hang low, will you get an undertow?
When they're resting on your lap, can your baby reach the tap?
Now you really needn't worry, if you get assistance in a hurry,
you can feed your baby if your boobs hang low.

Are your boobs too big for your babe to have a swig?
When he's looking for the fountain, will he have to climb
  a mountain?
Now you really needn't worry, if you get assistance in a hurry,
you can feed your baby if your boobs look big.

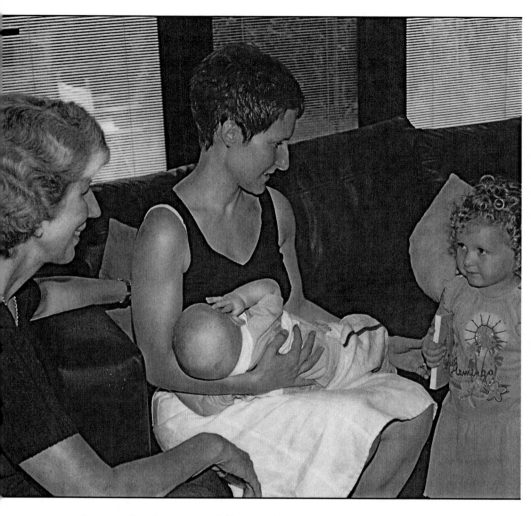

Are your boobs too small for your babe to have a ball?
Do you fear a low supply that'll leave him high and dry?
Now you really needn't worry, if you get assistance in a hurry,
you can feed your baby if your boobs look small.

Are your boobs too flat for your babe to guzzle at?
Will he get a proper tipple from an undercover nipple?
Now you really needn't worry, if you get assistance in a hurry,
you can feed your baby if your boobs look flat.

FIT TO BUST

*Are your boobs odd-sized, will your baby look surprised
after gorging on a ton, to find a tiny cherry bun?
Now you really needn't worry, if you get assistance in a hurry,
you can feed with boobs of any shape and size!*

Chapter 3

Great expectations

Preparing for motherhood

Many women in industrialised countries expect help in preparing for birth and breastfeeding, in contrast with those in developing countries, whose preparation consists mainly in living alongside other experienced women. While professional antenatal care is essential to prevent or treat medical complications, detailed instruction in feeding and bringing up baby may cause unnecessary anxiety, and disempower women.

Humans' caring instincts are reliant on hormones triggered by birth and early contact with their babies, and these skills are enhanced by observation of others and close support. Apes, elephants and dolphins also need others to help them. Cats are more independent.

This poem was given to me by an elderly retired midwife, whose name I have forgotten.

> *My pussy, Henrietta,*
> *is about to be a mummy;*
> *I wonder what it's like to have*
> *a playschool in your tummy?*
> *She looks around reproachfully*
> *as if to say, "You're rough!"*
> *But the kittens keep on playing –*
> *it must be really tough.*
>
> *Dad says she'll get her own back*
> *when she has them all, next week.*

She'll pin them down to wash their ears
and really make them squeak.
I look forward to stroking them,
and showing them to Gran;
but how will Pussy manage,
when she hasn't had a scan?

Antenatal classes and breastfeeding workshops can be very helpful, particularly for first-time mums. Chapter 17 has a number of resources for those who run them. Mothers may not remember a lot of instructions given during late pregnancy and early motherhood, but they can benefit from realistic information about how life changes with a little one.

Raising children is not an easy task, and lots of close support from family and friends will help. This song is dedicated to midwives and others who run preparation classes, and to parents who attend them. It's also an encouragement to get everyone singing, which is a great stress-buster!

Star thoroughfare
(tune: 'Scarborough Fair')

Are you going to have a wee child?
What a thrilling mountain to climb!
Remember these ideas we've compiled;
you may have an easier time.

Talk with your friends about what you may need:
help with housework, shifting the grime;
no matter how you're planning to feed,
babycare takes effort and time.

Find a companion for your Labour Day,
helping you at birthing to shine,
then hold your infant close, straight away;
he'll find nourishment, in good time.

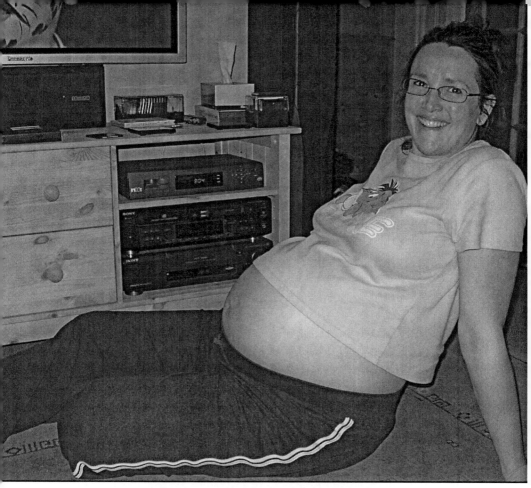

Planning to breastfeed? Good for you!

Follow your instincts and baby's desires;
you'll both know a joy that's sublime.
But seek good help, if this plan misfires,
then you'll have an easier time.

Nigel Rees's book *Babes and Sucklings* tells the story of a mother in late pregnancy whose three-year-old, finding her topless in her bedroom, asked, "What are those things?" She explained that they would provide milk for the new baby. He looked puzzled, and said, "How are you going to get the corks out?"[11]

Handy hint

Some women develop extra breast tissue during pregnancy, along a double line from the navel to the armpits – where other mammals such as dogs have their line of teats. What look like moles may turn out later to be mini-boobs. Usually any swelling or leakage after the birth subsides quickly, as that area isn't fully functional.

However, I did hear of one mother-to-be who had three extra growths alongside her breasts. They became uncomfortable in pregnancy, so she went along to Rigby and Peller for a made-to-measure bra. When the assistant asked her how she liked it, she replied, "It's great! It fits like a glove."

Homing instinct

Helping mothers to breastfeed starts with empowering them to give birth as naturally as possible. This preserves early feeding instincts. Home birth is a good option for many women, although they may need to push for it.

This song is dedicated to my friends Judy and Ruth. They both had their two children at home, and breastfed them for many months.

> ### There's no place like home
> (tune: 'Consider yourself' from *Oliver!*)
>
> *Deliver yourself at home!*
> *Deliver yourself, surrounded by family;*
> *contractions will be so strong*
> *we're sure – your – labour will not be long.*
>
> *Deliver yourself with ease!*
> *Deliver yourself on your own furniture;*
> *there's no-one to make a fuss*
> *if you – boo –, holler and swear and cuss.*
>
> *No need to pack your bags and trundle off to hospital,*
> *meeting people you don't know;*

*with all the lights and noise and strangers coming in and out,
labour's likely to be slow.*

*If factors of risk are small
and you're in the best of health,
with confidence and privacy and midwife's skill,
deliver your babe by yourself!*

Indie midwives: an endangered species

The UK government advises that the place of birth should be the mother's choice, as long as a midwife is in attendance. While home birth could be a safe option for many, there aren't enough NHS midwives to cover more than a small percentage. The answer could be to contract out to independent midwives, who at present work privately. However, these highly experienced practitioners have been struggling for years to get access to affordable insurance; without it, they may shortly be barred from practice. Visit the website of Independent Midwives UK for more information, and to sign their petition to ensure they do not become extinct.

Preparing for parenthood

The four voluntary breastfeeding support organisations have a range of literature on parenthood. One book, Naomi Stadlen's *What Mothers Do: Especially When It Looks Like Nothing*, is essential preparation not only for mothers, but for anyone involved in their support. It's deeply affirming of maternal achievements that usually go unrecognised and therefore unappreciated. Here's a flavour from the first chapter:

*Mothers live in a universe that has not been accurately
described. The right words have not been coined. It's hard
to find the words to communicate what "looking after my
baby" really means.*[12]

The following advice, extracted from 'Preparing for Parenthood' on various internet sites, goes some way to answer the question many mothers ask in the evening, 'What have I done all day?'

> *Women: To prepare for maternity, put on a dressing gown and stick a pillowcase filled with beans down the front. Leave it there for nine months. After nine months, take out 10 per cent of the beans.*

> *Men: To prepare for paternity, go to the local drug store, tip the contents of your wallet on the counter, and tell the pharmacist to help himself. Then go to the supermarket. Arrange to have your salary paid directly to their head office. Go home. Pick up the paper. Read it for the last time.*

> *Dressing small children is not as easy as it seems: first buy an octopus and a bag made out of loose mesh. Attempt to put the octopus into the bag so that none of the arms hang out. Time allowed for this: all morning.*

> *Hollow out a melon. Make a small hole in the side. Suspend it from the ceiling and swing it from side to side. Now get a bowl of soggy cereal shapes and attempt to spoon them into the swaying melon by pretending to be an aeroplane. Continue until half the cereal has gone. Tip the rest into your lap, making sure a lot of it falls on the floor. You are now ready to feed a 12-month-old baby.*

Baby-led weaning is the answer to this last challenge – see Chapter 10.

Chapter 4

Happy Birthday

Promoting normal birth and early breastfeeding

Happy birthday to you,
baby, warm wet and new;
Let me hold you, and enfold you –
what a beautiful view!

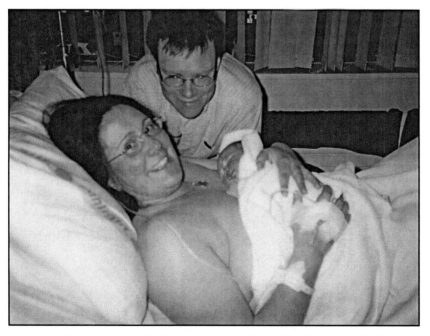

I was delighted to support Tania and James at Anna's birth as their doula

Keeping birth normal

During the last few years, the role of a 'doula' has become better known in the UK. Research shows that the presence of such a female companion, alongside a midwife, keeps the need for birth assistance low, and promotes breastfeeding.[13]

The increasing popularity of doulas is largely due to the work of obstetrician Dr Michel Odent, founder of the Primal Health Research Centre. He pioneered an empowering approach to childbirth (including waterbirths) in a French hospital in the 1970s, and has written extensively on birth and breastfeeding. On the occasion of his eightieth birthday I wrote this on his Facebook page:

> *Happy birthday, Michel,*
> *you've helped us excel*
> *in succeeding at breastfeeding*
> *and birth au naturel.*

Doulas do not replace midwives, but work alongside them to give mothers one-to-one care and protect the birth environment. The next song is dedicated to Michel and all the doulas he has trained, especially Heather Higgins whom I met when living in south-west London. Heather is also a trainee BFC, and the mother of two breastfed children. She confirms that the feelings I've described here are authentic.

Birth plan
(tune: 'Close every door to me' from *Joseph and the Amazing Technicolour Dreamcoat*)

Close every door to me,
chatter no more to me,
give me a midwife who trusts in my power.

4. HAPPY BIRTHDAY

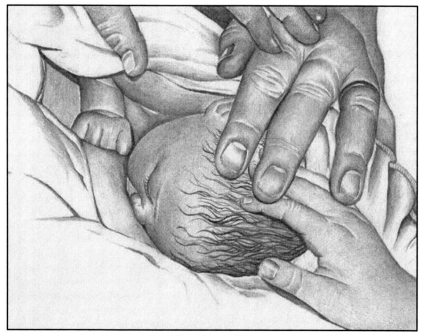

Family welcome   © Heidi Scarfone

Leave us in privacy,
working in harmony,
journeying on to the ultimate hour.

For this time is important
to establish my labour-day;
in silence and darkness
my fears melt away.

I'm in a twilight zone,
distant, but not alone;
soon comes the storm-surge but I won't recoil.
For I know I'll be strong,
and before very long
my babe will be tasting the fruit of my toil.

The fruit of women's toil is indeed precious, although babies may not enjoy it for some hours, if at all. But they would, if they could choose.

Get me to the breast on time
(tune: 'Get me to the church on time' from *My Fair Lady*)

I'll be delivered in the morning,
when from this cosy womb I'll climb;
keep me with Mummy, serene on her tummy,
and get me to the breast on time.

I want a haven safe and warming,
where I can meet that Mum of mine;
no need to weigh me, on soft bosom lay me,
and get me to the breast on time.

   If I am weepy, skin contact's best;
   If I am sleepy, give me hand-expressed!

So when I'm delivered in the morning,
my birthday meal will taste sublime;
richness and sweetness, with joy in completeness,
so get me to the breast, get me to the breast,
for my sake, get me to the breast on time.

Skincubators

During an online discussion about reducing reliance on incubators, midwife Helena Bull came up with this brilliant word for parents providing skin contact for newborns. (See p170.)

The practice of carrying near-naked premature babies inside the mother's clothes for prolonged periods, termed Kangaroo Mother Care, was started in Colombia in the late 1970s. Research by the South African paediatrician Dr Nils Bergman has shown that KMC is safer for many vulnerable newborns than incubator care. (Fathers can also get involved; see Chapter 16 for more information.) Studies of full-term babies also show that early skin contact calms the stress reactions of birth, and releases the 'love hormone' oxytocin in both baby and mother.[14]

Skin to skin

(tune: 'Dancing cheek to cheek' from *Top Hat*)

Heaven, I'm in heaven, with a precious little body by my chin,
and I quite forget the pain that I've been in
when I'm lying with my baby, skin to skin.

Heaven, we're in heaven; after giving birth this feeling is the best,
as my baby starts to nuzzle at my breast,
while we lie in peace together, chest to chest.

Being born is very shocking, now my baby needs to rest,
and the safest, warmest place to lie is underneath my vest.
I can always give him comfort every time he seems distressed,
we'll embrace each other skin to skin, and both feel very blessed

Bonding, we are bonding, and our new relationship
*   can now begin;*
something wonderful is happening within
when I'm lying with my baby, skin to skin.

Breast stroke

The instinct of babies born without medical intervention to find their natural source of food has only recently become apparent. If left undisturbed on his mother's chest, the newborn makes arm and leg movements akin to swimming, to move purposefully to the breast and take his first meal, usually within an hour. You can see this skill, shared with all baby mammals, in YouTube clips of films made in India and Sweden, entitled or linked to Breast Crawl. But these clips do not show maternal instinctive actions, as the mothers are passive; the Indian mother is lying completely flat. This may be because the films were made to show that breastfed babies do not need the adult control necessary in other forms of infant feeding.

However, normal breastfeeding is an equal partnership between mother and baby. The concept of 'Biological Nurturing', described by research midwife Suzanne Colson PhD, arose from observation of instinctive behaviour in both baby and mother.* Dr Colson's work has been picked up by several breastfeeding authorities, most notably LCs Nancy Mohrbacher and Kathy Kendall-Tackett, authors of *Breastfeeding Made Simple: Seven Natural Laws for Breastfeeding Mothers*. In 2005, Natural Law #1 stated: 'Babies Are Hardwired to Breastfeed'. In the second edition of 2010, this now reads 'Babies and Mothers Are Hardwired to Breastfeed'.

Specialists often refer to the mother and newborn as a 'dyad', or pair, recognising that what affects one is likely to affect the other. The first feed is an integral part of the birthing process, providing a wonderful welcome for both parties.

Breastfeed
(tune: 'Downtown' sung by Petula Clark)

What do you think a baby wants to do most when
he has just been born?

---

* See Chapter 5.

4. HAPPY BIRTHDAY

Breastfeed.

How can he best recover, when from his mother's
*   womb he's rudely torn?*
Breastfeed.

The scent of mother's bosom is a comforting reminder
of flavours that he's savoured in the life he's left behind
*   – a haven of rest.*

The beat of her loving heart,
the tender warmth of her breast
will surely help him to start
his first breastfeed,
soothing and strengthening breastfeed,
tasty and welcoming breastfeed,
life-giving, love-making breastfeed.

How can a mother give the tenderest welcome to
*   her newborn child?*
Breastfeed.
How can she feel that all her struggle in birthing
*   him has been worthwhile?*
Breastfeed.

For 40 weeks she's carried him to feed and pacify him,
and now her body still can comfort him, and satisfy his hunger
and thirst.

This time should be never cut short,
to hold him closely at first,
giving space to support her to breastfeed,
lovingly, peacefully breastfeed,
gladly, excitedly breastfeed,
calmly and joyfully breastfeed.

Chapter 5

A new life together

From pregnancy to motherhood and womb to world

New parents encounter many changes to their lives, and have to learn new skills. Most mothers need particular encouragement in the early days. This song was inspired by the Be A Star campaign mentioned in Chapter 1.

> **This new mum's a star!**
> (tune: 'This old man, he played one')
>
> *This new mum, on day one,*
> *thrilled to bits that labour's done,*
> *holds her newborn to her loving breast,*
> *then enjoys a well-earned rest.*
>
> *This new mum, on day two,*
> *learning quickly what to do,*
> *feeds her babe as often as she can,*
> *staves off jaundice* by this plan.*
>
> *This new mum, on day three,*
> *finds she's now a double D,*
> *leaking milk and bursting into tears,*
> *needing hugs to calm her fears.*

---

* Mild newborn jaundice (yellowing of the baby's skin) is normal; early feeding reduces the risk of harmful jaundice.

This new mum, on day four,
feeling anxious and unsure,
needs some help when baby starts to yell,
but she's really doing well.

This new mum, on day five,
knows that she can now survive;
friends and family give a loud "Hurrah!"
This new mum's the greatest STAR!

Cherry Ripe

A useful way for mothers to know that their baby is well attached to the breast, apart from being pain-free, is to check that the nipple looks no different after the feed. However, one mother told me that her health visitor thought the baby was attaching correctly, despite her pain, as her nipples came out shaped like an 'orthodontic' bottle teat.

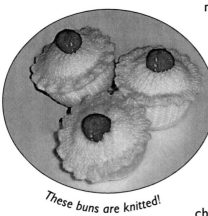

These buns are knitted!

Midwife and LC Carol Walton explains to mothers that when the baby releases the nipple, it should look like a cherry on an iced bun – soft, short and round (though not bright red). Carol is now the proud owner of jewellery, greetings cards, mugs, plates and other items showing cherries on buns, given by grateful parents.

Hospital experiences

Life on a hospital postnatal ward has changed enormously since I was born. My mother was in a nursing home for a fortnight, leaving her sister and my father to look after my siblings, aged four and two. When asked how she spent her time, she replied, "I knitted a shawl!" At the start of my midwifery training in 1974, the rules had just changed to allow first-time mothers to go home early after a normal birth, on the seventh day. Experienced mothers could leave within two days, with home visits by the district midwife. Caesarean-born babies and their mothers had to stay at least ten days. It was common for babies to go to the ward nursery overnight, and have glucose water or formula if they cried.

Now, mothers and babies are generally kept together, and frequent breastfeeding is encouraged, if not always facilitated. Formula feeds may be available on request, but in some maternity units parents are asked to bring in their own supplies. This can give staff the chance to explain how to bottle-feed as safely as possible. New mothers are given Bounty packs containing adverts and free samples of laundry products and non-recyclable nappies; fortunately, 'first stage' formula is now excluded. However, giving their contact details assures mothers of a cascade of adverts from babyfood companies six months later. An alternative is available in the 'Mama Pack', which promotes breastfeeding and environmentally friendly products such as washable nappies.*

These days, the new family is discharged home as soon as possible, partly because of a chronic shortage of midwives. Many leave a few hours after the birth, often without having enough knowledge or experience in feeding to ensure that all goes well at home. Those who need to stay may find it a noisy, stressful and lonely experience.

I wrote this song after seeing a Channel 4 TV documentary, 'Undercover Mother', which revealed poor postnatal care after a caesarean birth in a North London hospital. It all rang horribly true.

---

* See p252.

FIT TO BUST

Let me go home
(tune: 'Sloop John B' sung by the Beach Boys)

I'm in a maternity ward,
my calls are being ignored,
around the rooms in search of midwives I roam;

> **Refrain:**
> *I wanna go home, why don't they let me go home, yeah yeah,*
> *I feel so weary, I wanna go home.*

Last night all the babies roared,
my pulse and blood pressure soared,
I now feel as lively as a gardener's gnome;

> **Refrain**

My dignity's gone overboard,
as a woman, I feel a fraud,
you'd think that my hair had never encountered a comb;

> **Refrain**

My breasts are as hard as a board
despite being thoroughly pawed;
they're massive but useless, like the Millennium Dome;

> **Refrain**

Support when we're home is assured,
so for freedom I've begged and implored,
and now in despair, at the mouth I'm starting to foam;

> **Last refrain:**
> *They've let me go home! They've let me go home!*
> *I feel so happy – we're now going home!*

5. A NEW LIFE TOGETHER

Home help

Once mothers and babies are at home, they may need extra help with feeding. Midwives and health visitors well trained in breastfeeding support are invaluable, although finding the time to spend with new parents is a challenge. Peer supporters, with fewer conflicting tasks, can make all the difference to a new mother's life; see Chapter 17.

HV and LC Sharon Breward tells of a generation gap she encountered while helping a young mother at home:

> I was at a young mum's house one morning. Big breastfeeding crisis, mum had had a terrible night, needed to go back to bed and feed lying down (stitches etc – you know how it is) to settle the babe. I helped her into a comfy position on her side, and it seemed that we needed a little wedge to lift the breast off the mattress a bit, so she could better see baby attaching. I usually ask for a tea towel to roll up, but as we were upstairs this wasn't easiest thing to access, so I asked her for a clean pair of knickers. "They're in me top drawer," she said. I opened the drawer to find it full of the smallest G-strings I'd ever seen, and certainly not the sturdy Marks & Sparks jobs I had envisaged! I held one up and said, "D'you know, I just don't think this is going to do the trick." Well! The mum laughed so much – did her a power of good and me too!

Cream crackers

In the interests of scientific research, Sharon has sampled nipple creams to see which was most palatable. She says:

> I put them all on a bit of cream cracker and ate them at hourly intervals – one repeated terribly – worse than cucumber – for some reason though, The Lancet was not interested in my findings.

Despite this lack of interest, Sharon was recognised in the 2008 Queen's Birthday Honours with an MBE. She certainly is a Marvellous Breastfeeding Encourager.

Laid-back breastfeeding

Of course, if women get the right support from the start, they won't encounter so many difficulties. For years, breastfeeding advice has commonly included a list of instructions, because both mothers and babies apparently have to learn how to breastfeed. Advice on 'position and attachment' depicts women sitting bolt upright or lying on their side, holding the baby with one or both arms and lining up their baby 'nose to nipple'. (These pictures usually show an observer's view and not the mother's view.) Although such positions can be really helpful, there is no evidence that they are the only ones that work.

However, research has now been done into which positions work best. Dr Suzanne Colson, a La Leche League Leader and former midwifery lecturer, conducted video research for her PhD, awarded in 2006. She uses the term 'biological nurturing' (BN) to describe a range of breastfeeding postures for the mother, and positions for the baby, which release instinctive behaviour in both.[15] In BN, instead of trying to follow traditional 'position and attachment' instructions, mothers lean back comfortably and place their babies face down on their chest, just as many of them did right after birth. This position triggers feeding reflexes and helps babies take the breast spontaneously. Mothers can relax with their head and body well supported, and have both hands free - and don't have to sit on a line of needlework!*

Being in one's right mind

BN is not just about feeding; it promotes the release of pleasurable hormones in both mother (or other carer) and baby, by enhancing the activity of the intuitive, right side of the brain. This part of the

---

* The feeding reflexes are seen in all babies, however they are fed, but some practical adjustments are needed for bottle-feeding.

5. A NEW LIFE TOGETHER

brain is essential for emotional connections, and is dominant in newborns. In mature women, logical, left-brained activity is subdued in late pregnancy and early motherhood; this may be because empathy and intuition are more important than logic in developing a caring bond with the baby. That's why a long list of instructions of how to breastfeed may not be helpful.

Instead of giving such detailed instructions, Dr Colson recommends that maternity staff encourage mothers to hold their babies in BN for at least the first three days. The hormones released help the baby adapt to the world with minimal stress, and enhance the mother's own instincts, making both early and ongoing breastfeeding more likely. This self-service approach has transformed my practice, and the experience of many mothers and their helpers.

BN may be the only way disabled mothers can breastfeed unaided. Alison Lapper, the artist born with no arms, was shown using BN

© *Suzanne Colson*

to feed her son Parys in the first series of the BBC documentary *Child of Our Time*.

BN positions and postures build on earlier research by Dr Colson examining the baby's adaptation from his inner to outer world. Her article 'From Womb to World', written in 2002 for *Midwifery Today*, can be read online.[16] It inspired this poem, which is based on the song 'Out of My Dreams' from *Oklahoma!*.

From womb to world

Out of my womb and into my arms
a child has newly come;
as I hold him, safe from harm,
our joy has now begun.
In a caress, reclining in peace,
our instincts are preserved;
bonds of love are made,
my infant finds his food,
attentive but unafraid,
with all distress subdued.

Good attachment to the breast, also known as a good latch, is the key to successful breastfeeding. My latch key (opposite) might help mothers and babies to get started.

For more information on feeding challenges such as slow weight gain, tongue-tie, and mastitis, and the support that BFCs and LCs can give, see Chapter 17.

What goes in....

In my work as a midwife and then Infant Feeding Adviser, I encountered mothers every day who were struggling with feeding. Many were worried about how much the baby was taking. I found that the best way to judge intake was to look at what came out the other end.

5. A NEW LIFE TOGETHER

Lean back comfortably
Allow baby to rest on your body
Take off outer clothing
Check breast is soft for baby to grasp
Help baby very gently

Keep asking for help if it hurts
Express milk if necessary
Your nipples should look the same after feeding.

The five days of feeding
(tune: 'The twelve days of Christmas')

On the first day of feeding, your babe will give to you
a wee and a sticky black poo.

On the second day of feeding, your babe will give to you
two little wees and a less sticky, thinner dark poo.

On the third day of feeding, your babe will give to you

three little wees, two little burps and a big greeny-browny soft poo.

*On the fourth day of feeding, your babe will give to you
four little wees, three little farts, two little burps and a nice runny toffee-brown poo.*

*On the fifth day of feeding, your babe will give to you
five bi-ig wees;
four little farts,
three big burps,
two overflows,
and a large golden mustard-seed poo!*

The Happy Knappy

To illustrate expected changes in output, I have created a knitted modern-shaped nappy (see opposite) with five coloured circles attached, ranging from black through greeny-brown to golden yellow. See Chapter 18 for more details.

Rubbish removal

In the early 1990s a concern for the environment, helped by the development of easy-care fabrics, brought washable nappies back into fashion. I used to keep several modern varieties in my community midwife's bag (unused), to show parents how attractive and practical they could be.

The slogan of the Real Nappy Campaign at that time was 'Real nappies don't cost the Earth – anything else is just rubbish'. It inspired the next song, which came into my mind almost complete at 1.30am one night as I was settling in bed. Having no paper to hand, I scribbled it down on a box of tissues and finished it the next day. It is dedicated to Eirlys Penn, who was shortlisted for Londoner of the Year in the late 1990s for her work with the Real Nappy Network.

Thanks to her and many others, more children are now enjoying proper nappies, just as I did!

Nappy Talk

(tune: 'Happy talk' from *South Pacific*)

Refrain
Nappy talk, keep talking nappy talk;
talk about baby's pee and poo.
You've got to throw away excreta every day,
but you needn't throw the nappy too.

Single-use napp-ies
use up lots of trees,
needing chlorine bleach to make them white.
Each contains elastic,

chemicals and plastic,
which won't rot in any landfill site.

Refrain (may be omitted)

Nappies made of cotton
should not be forgotten;
soft and comfy, they don't cost the Earth;
kinder to the botty,
faster route to potty –
could be less than two years from the birth!

Refrain (may be omitted)

If you wash at home,
there's no need to moan;
notice how much heavier your purse is.
If you're short of time,
or can't face the grime,
use your local nappy-washing service!

Last refrain
Nappy talk, keep talking nappy talk;
talk about baby's pee and poo.
You've got to throw away excreta every day,
but you needn't throw the nappy too;
if you use real nappies there'll be less to throw away,
and you'll save the Earth, and money too!

> Breastfeeding and real nappies make babies green at both ends.

An even greener option is to discard the nappy altogether. Close contact enhances a carer's awareness of the baby's reflex activity in both feeding and elimination. An internet search on 'nappy-free alternatives' gives more information on this practice, which is perfectly normal in Pakistan. Women would slip out of church to dangle their babies under the bush just outside, with an encouraging "swswsws". Caution was needed when travelling by train, as a mother on the upper bunk might hold out her baby at any time without warning.

A cry for help

The early days aren't just about feeding, of course. During this time, parents get to know their new arrivals, and learn how to meet all their needs. This song was written as an antidote to the advice of childcare 'gurus' who claim that babies shouldn't be picked up when they cry. The subject is discussed further in Chapter 22.

> **Close to you**
> (tune: 'Close to You' by The Carpenters)
>
> *Why do babes always start to weep*
> *when you hope that they'll sleep?*
> *Can't you see? They long to be close to you.*
>
> **Why do they seem to be afraid*
> *when in cots they are laid?*
> *You'll agree, they want to be close to you.*
>
> *From the day that they were born*
> *they've needed your protection,*
> *to be comforted and safe from all alarms,*
> *so they call for close connection*
> *till they're gathered in a parent's loving arms.*

---

* If singing with karaoke tape, at the reprise repeat from * in the first verse to continue

FIT TO BUST

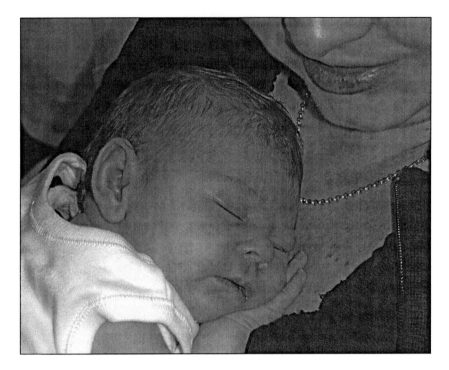

So each time babies call to you,
you will know what to do.
Heed their plea, they need to be close to you!
Heed their plea, they need to be close to you!

Chapter 6

Sleeping on the job

Caring for babies at night

Midnight feasts

It is normal for young babies to feed around the clock. Their fuel tanks are small, and the recommended fuel of human milk, being low in protein, is quickly used up. Frequent contact with parents also assures babies' safety, and builds up connections in their brains.

Many parents are advised to give artificial milk supplements or babyfood before the recommended six months of exclusive breast-feeding, in the mistaken belief that this will encourage the baby to 'go through the night'. Popular childcare books may claim that

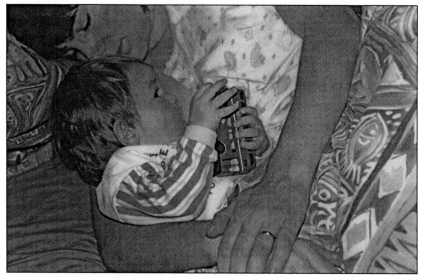

Transport of delight

children should learn to sleep alone, and for long spells, from an early age. But studies show that the common British practice of 'training' or conditioning young babies to sleep alone is harmful, because any separation from parents increases stress hormones.

Margot Sunderland, Director of Education at the Centre for Child Mental Health in London, urges parents to sleep with their babies until they are at least five years old. In her fascinating book *The Science of Parenting* (also entitled *What Every Parent Needs to Know*), she says that co-sleeping makes children more likely to grow into calm, healthy adults.

Sharing a bed encourages more breastfeeding, and helps the mother to sleep better too. But this is a controversial subject. Alongside growing evidence that solitary infant sleep is risky, studies into sudden infant death show that some co-sleeping practices, for example sharing a sofa, are also dangerous.

Blanket disapproval of bedsharing

Because of fears that any bedsharing must be dangerous, some authorities have attempted to outlaw it. But a blanket ban isn't safe for two main reasons: many parents take their babies into bed during the night anyway; and those who avoid doing so may end up falling asleep with them on the sofa. It's safer to give parents clear, evidence-based guidance on what constitutes safe bed-sharing, such as the leaflet 'Sharing a bed with your baby', available on the Baby Friendly Initiative website. Recent research by Dr Helen Ball at the Parent-Infant Sleep Lab in Durham University shows that breast-feeding mothers act protectively towards their bedsharing infants, even in sleep.

The following song is dedicated to BF advocate and cartoonist Kate Evans, in admiration for her hilarious drawings showing the differences between bedsharing and using a cot. Visit the website of her book *The Food of Love*, and click on the link 'Breastfeed in your sleep'.

Mammary
(tune: 'Memory' from *Cats*)

Midnight, not a sound from the nursery;
is my baby still sleeping? Should I go and make sure?
In the moonlight, the duvet's pulled away from my feet,
and my bed-mate begins to snore.

Restless, I am fitfully dozing,
for I know I'll be woken by a pitiful wail;
I remember the time I knew what energy was,
now I'm feeling old and frail.

After feeds, my babe's content, and off to sleep she is falling;
I embrace her, in the cot I place her, but soon she will be bawling.
Hear her! It's not easy to leave her
all alone in the darkness where she'll bitterly weep;
let me fetch her, and then we'll know what happiness is;
it's a threesome, fast asleep.

Bedtime stories

Story-telling is a universal way of sharing important truths. LC Sarah Brown is a keen advocate, and wrote this one for Treasure Chest (abridged with permission).

Breastfeeding while asleep

During a walking holiday in Spain, I told the other ramblers that I was a midwife who specialised in infant feeding, especially breastfeeding support. This was met with many stories from men and women who wanted to share their experiences of feeding their children. One story stayed with me more than the others did.

The woman told me her husband was very keen for her to breastfeed her children, but she didn't know why until later. When the first baby was born in hospital, she became very tired when woken to feed her baby. The first night home she drifted off into a wonderful deep sleep, and woke in the morning to find an exhausted partner. He had paced the house with a hungry baby, as he couldn't wake his wife – she just rolled over and went back to sleep. Eventually, in desperation, he opened her nightdress and plonked the baby on her breast. The baby fed well on both sides and had another feed later, but the mother had no recollection of this when she finally awoke.

The night feeds continued in this way with both children for months. The father's original reason for championing breastfeeding was to get a good night's sleep while his wife breastfed...

6. SLEEPING ON THE JOB

Let's spend the night together
(tune: 'All through the night')

Mother hopes for lazy dreaming
*   all through the night.*
But her newborn baby's screaming
*   all through the night.*
Fed and burped, with change of nappy,
in his cot he should be happy,
but he's still a grumpy chappy
*   all through the night.*

Once her baby lay inside her
*   all through the night.*
Now he longs to stay beside her
*   all through the night.*
Mother wakes before he's crying,
tasty milk she's soon supplying,
cuddled close, in peace they're lying
*   all through the night.*

What is normal?

Bedsharing is common in countries such as China, where the occurence of sudden infant death is very low. In Pakistan, I never heard of babies being found dead in bed with no apparent cause, despite the fact that most of them slept close to the mother. It was common to see the whole family sleeping in one room, with at least two per bed. (One of the hospital staff was amazed to learn that I had a room AND a bed to myself.) Since my return, I have seen how mother's sleep and baby's weight gain may both be improved by increased closeness at night.

When babies are tucked up next to mum, they can have really sweet dreams.

White Breakfast for Baby
(tune: 'White Christmas')

I'm dreaming of a white breakfast,
just like the feast I had last night;
what a lovely tipple, when open zip'll
reveal an appetising sight.

I'm dreaming of a white breakfast
and every creamy pint I'll pull;
may its flavour be natural,
and may all my breakfast-cups be full.

This next song was inspired by Deborah Jackson's book about the normality of co-sleeping, *Three in a Bed*. The bed needs to be Royal Family-size!

Five in a Bed
(tune: 'Ten in the bed')

There was Mum in the bed and the baby said,
"Roll over! Roll over!"
So she rolled right over and the babe jumped in,
there were two in the bed and the little boy said,
"Roll over! Roll over!"
So they both rolled over and the boy jumped in,
there were three in the bed and the little girl said,
"Roll over! Roll over!"
So they all rolled over and the girl jumped in,
there were four in the bed and the father said,
"Roll over! Roll over!"
So they all rolled over and Dad jumped in,
there were five in the bed and they cuddled and said,
"We're in clover! We're in clover!"

Chapter 7

Full stream ahead

The first six months

This song is dedicated to my LCGB colleagues who joined in with gusto when I sang it karaoke-style, with actions, at our annual conference in 2004. It's also performed on YouTube by members of Cuidiu, the Irish Childbirth Trust.

Big feeder
(tune: 'Big spender' from *Sweet Charity*)

The minute you came to my arms,
I could see you were a babe with a mission,
a real big feeder;
head bobbing, mouth ajar –
say, wouldn't you like to wait until I open my bra?
So let me display all my charms,
get a let-down, so my milk is flowing free.
Hey big feeder! Have a little meal on me.

Would you like to have Mum,
Mum, Mum
fill your bottomless – tum,
tum?
I can give you some
(boom boom) foremilk!
I can give you some
(boom boom) hindmilk!

Prêt à boire Sophia and George on a French beach

All together now!

The minute you came to my arms,
I could see you were a babe with a mission,
a real big feeder,
head bobbing, mouth ajar –
say, wouldn't you like to wait until I open my bra?

So let me display all my charms,
get a let-down, so my milk is flowing free.
Hey big feeder!
Hey big feeder!
Hey big feeder!
Have a little meal on me – (count six more beats) –
Yeah!

Carry on as normal

In many parts of the world, babies are carried around all the time, attached to their mother's body. According to Dr Nils Bergman of Kangaroo Mother Care fame, this is normal behaviour. He describes the mother as the baby's natural habitat, as humans are 'carry mammals' like apes and kangaroos. He also points out that we have more in common with marsupials in regard to childcare, because our babies are much more vulnerable at birth than their primate cousins.

Professor Narvaez of Notre Dame University, mentioned earlier, lists six behaviours common to our hunter-gatherer ancestors. Two such aspects of childcare are described:

Lots of positive touch – as in no spanking – but nearly
constant carrying, cuddling and holding.

Prompt response to baby's fusses and cries. This means
meeting a child's needs before they get upset and the brain
is flooded with toxic chemicals. Warm, responsive caregiving

like this keeps the infant's brain calm in the years it is
forming its personality and response to the world.[17]

Love changes everything

Professor Narvaez's advice matches what Dr Margot Sunderland says
in *The Science of Parenting*. She shows how parents can engage with
their babies in very practical ways, providing security and comfort
until the child is able to regulate his or her feelings later on. If children
don't get such care, their higher brain can't develop and remains
stunted for life. This can be clearly seen in brain scans of babies who
suffered severe neglect in Romanian orphanages in the 1990s.

The way in which early affection maximises the brain's potential
is described in fascinating detail by psychotherapist Sue Gerhardt, in
her book *Why Love Matters*. This approach stands in stark contrast
with the Babywise programme of scheduled feeding and harsh disci-
pline advocated by American author Gary Ezzo, and condemned by
many childcare specialists.

Many people think that babies shouldn't feed frequently. But if
they wrote down the times they put something into their mouths,
they would realise that it's normal for all of us to have something to
eat or drink every two or three hours. Moreover, whenever we eat
with family and friends, our relationships have a chance to deepen.
The hormones released at such times (as long as they are happy
occasions!) create strong bonds of love, and increase our pleasure.
It may help tired mothers to remember that every time their baby
nurses, he or she is growing brain as well as brawn!

Here's a song from the baby's point of view, to the tune of 'A Nice
Cup of Tea' as sung by Binnie Hale on YouTube.

Interlock around the clock

I like a nice mummy feed at day's dawning
just to give me what I need,

and at nine and eleven, well my idea of heaven
is a nice mummy feed.

I like a nice mummy feed during dinner,
and a nice mummy feed after tea,
then a snack at supper's right,
and in the middle of the night
it's so easy to please me!

Service station

In Pakistan, women carry babies in their arms and offer the breast frequently. When attending church there, I noticed that the start of the minister's talk would prompt the rustling of many shawls, so that everyone could peacefully drink in the sermon.

By contrast, thousands of babycare products in industrialised countries are designed to keep children and parents apart. For example, most pushchairs and buggies – certainly the most affordable ones – do not even allow frequent eye contact between baby and carer, unlike old-fashioned prams. The growing use of slings bucks these trends. A vicar I once met on holiday told me that when she gave birth soon after her ordination, a friend gave her four slings in colours to match her liturgical vestments. The next song celebrates baby-wearing, which is now really cool.[18]

My favourite sling
(tune: 'My favourite things' from *The Sound of Music*)

Softer than cradles and baskets of Moses,
perfect for holding my babe as he dozes;
he will know luxury fit for a king,
when he is laid in my favourite sling.

Good for the housework or feeding in public,
cosy and comfy with washable fabric,

7. FULL STREAM AHEAD

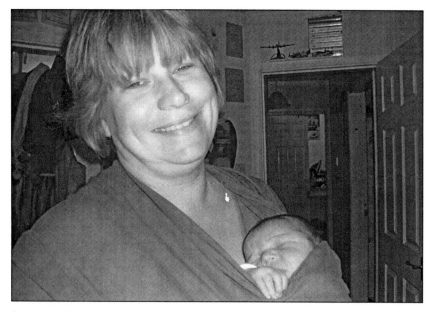

Doris and 4-day-old Tj

fully adjustable, using a ring (or string!) –
I'm undismayed, in my favourite sling.

When my babe bites, when my boobs sting,
when the cries won't cease,
I simply assemble my favourite sling,
and then we have perfect peace!

The next song celebrates the mutual delight enjoyed when feeding is going well.

How it's meant to be
(tune: 'Tea for Two')

Milk for you is milk from me,
it's good for breakfast, lunch and tea,
for dinner, bedtime snack and midnight feast;
fragrant and soothing, it's nicely presented

in softest containers that Nature invented
with taste ever-changing, in perfect amounts released – so –

Day will break, and you'll awake
and milk I'll make for you to take,
we'll have a break, and then relax in peace;
basking in tranquillity, delight for you and joy for me,
for this is how our life is meant to be.

When you wake from restful sleep,
a luscious harvest you will reap,
a meal that's perfectly digestible.
First there's the starter, so light and delicious,
and then comes the main course, it's fresh and nutritious;
a creamy dessert means that now you're completely full – so –

You can sit upon my knee,
I'll gaze at you, you'll gaze at me,
we'll share a time of joyful company.
Precious baby, heaven-sent,
within my arms you rest content,
for this is how our life is meant to be.

However, this life isn't usually neat and tidy. Belinda Evans, creator of some of the wonderful cartoons in this book, told me her memory of nursing a young baby:

> *I recall NEVER being able to eat my food when it was still hot … and in desperation slurping spaghetti bolognaise across my sleepily sucking baby's head and leaving trails of tomatoey sauce across her cellular blanket and babygro … terrible mother!*

When there's more than one baby, particular challenges arise, and much help is needed. Mothers of multiples may be told that breast-feeding won't be possible, but even women with only one functional

7. FULL STREAM AHEAD

The bosom of the family *Fully breast-fed triplets in Brazil*

breast can feed twins. The inspiring story of one such mother, 'One Breast is Enough', can be read online.[19]

Breastfeeding and work

During the first few months, many women return to work. For some this spells the end of their breastfeeding relationship, as there are many obstacles to its continuation. The next song is dedicated to those wonderful mothers who do carry on while working, and to all employers who make it possible.*

The Daily Express
(tune: 'Wouldn't it be loverly' from *My Fair Lady*)

All I want is a room somewhere,
far away from the office glare,
with soft and comfy chair -
O, wouldn't it be loverly?

---

* See www.direct.gov.uk 'Statutory Maternity Leave: returning to work'

FIT TO BUST

*I like my milk from my mum, not just from any old cow**

Soap and towel to wash and dry,
tasty snack and a drink nearby,
the door locked if I'm shy -
O, wouldn't it be loverly?

Pumping loverly milk, delightful and digestible;
I would never stop until me bottle's completely full.

Now tomorrow me babe won't need
bovine brew for the midday feed,
if all my plans succeed;
O, wouldn't it be loverly?

---

* Caption from Lactivist materials *www.lactivist.co.uk*

Chapter 8

Dad's the word

The vital role of fathers

For the last four decades or so, men have been made welcome at the birth, rather than banished until after the baby's arrival. The newborn will need comfort, so if his mother is unable to hold him immediately, the next best person is his father. One woman whom I helped to give birth felt too unwell for a cuddle, so her partner held their son inside his shirt. By the time she had recovered, the baby was rooting around on Dad's chest. When put with his mother, he went straight to her breast. She later told me that her partner had loved holding the baby, and was now in charge of all the nappies.

This limerick by Ann Daniels, retired midwife, was sent to LC Hilary Myers.

> *Now fathers are urged to undress –*
> *no jumper, no shirt or a vest.*
> *It's to help them to bond,*
> *but will baby feel conned*
> *if no milk is forthcoming*
> *from breast?*

Men in Northern Ireland are left in no doubt about the importance of their role in helping women to nurse their babies.

This poster was used in Breastfeeding Awareness Week in 2007, and appeared in the sports sections of local press and in the male washrooms of over 200 entertainment venues across the country.

© Health Promotion Agency for Northern Ireland

Knight Nurses

Close contact with babies increases caring and calm behaviour in males as well as females, partly because of the release of the hormone prolactin. I saw this in a TV programme about silverback gorillas. A three-year-old, abandoned by her mother, was keeping close to her father. Although he didn't hold her closely to keep her warm at night or feed her, as her mother would have done, he obviously had a loving bond with her. Alex Strong, the father of my godson Thomas and his brother William, displays even more caring behaviour.

Batty milkmen

It is in fact possible for males taking care of infants to produce milk, as the breast is basically the same in males and females, and prolactin causes milk secretion. However, the Dayak fruit bat of Malaysia is apparently the only mammal in which male lactation is a normal occurrence, albeit at a much lower volume than in females. It does also happen occasionally in humans. The fascinating and hilarious book *Fresh Milk* by Fiona Giles has several stories of nursing fathers.

This song is for all fathers who want to bond with their breastfed baby, and for the mothers who rely on their help.

> ***Don't panic!*** (tune: Dad's Army theme)
>
> *Who do you think mothers need when they are nursing,*
> *when they're feeling tired and glum?*
> *Here are the boys who can help you in the night,*
> *here are the boys who will make you feel all right;*
> *so prod them awake every time you feel like cursing,*
> *then your stress you'll overcome.*

FIT TO BUST

Dads are good at soothing babies, so that mums can rest;
what a treat to lie upon a warm and hairy chest.
So just bear in mind, when your little ones are nursing,
they need Dad as well as Mum!

A young mother found herself sitting by an off-duty airline pilot on a short-haul flight. He was friendly but tactful, turning away whenever she fed her baby. On arrival, he gallantly helped with her luggage and remarked, 'You have a fine son, but what an appetite!' She explained that her midwife had suggested nursing at take-off and landing, to keep the baby's ears comfortable. He commented ruefully, 'I wish I'd known. All these years, I've just been sucking mints.'

Chapter 9

Out in the open

Feeding away from home

Posy Simmonds' witty cartoon of 1984 is still being acted out in many places.

Cartoon by kind permission of Posy Simmonds and The Guardian *newspaper*

Why should women hide this life-enhancing activity, and why should anyone suggest they decamp to a public convenience? Some do prefer privacy, but may not be able to find a comfortable – or sanitary – place to feed. One of my pet hates is the bottle sign outside many baby-changing rooms. As most of these places are totally unsuitable for any kind of feeding, the bottle merely symbolises babyhood. And does it refer to delivery or collection of fluid?

Off topic

While we're on the subject of public conveniences, here's a song inspired by an article on the internet entitled 'Why Women Take A Long Time When Nature Calls'. This explains to the uninitiated all the reasons for women's lengthy comfort stops, and why they often go in pairs. The song is dedicated to the vanishing race of conscientious lavatory attendants.

> ### Bide a wee
> (tune:'Dad's Army' theme)
>
> *"Why do you take such a long time in the Ladies?"*
> *This is what our menfolk say.*
> *We're not the boys who need only to unzip,*
> *we're not the boys who don't worry if they drip;*
> *so when they enquire why we're taking simply ages,*
> *here's the cause of our delay.*
>
> *We make sure the pan receives each penny as it lands,*
> *carefully replace our clothes, and *ALWAYS WASH OUR HANDS*.*

So please recollect, as we queue up in the Ladies,
why we need a lengthy stay!

... at half speed

Out for lunch

Women of older generations may query the need to feed a young baby outside the home; they generally stayed indoors until the baby could go longer between feeds. But today's mothers enjoy going out with their babies, although many feel worried about providing comfort without drawing negative comments. To alleviate this anxiety, BFCs and LCs can help by giving information about local breastfeeding friendly shops and stores.*

This cartoon now decorates an LCGB promotional mug, with the caption 'lactation consultants help mums and babies stay connected'.[20]

Cover girls

A whole industry has grown up around this concern. Clothing varies from nursing tops with slits or flaps to massive tents which completely hide the baby too.** But a simple, inexpensive wrap can work just as well.

---

* See the NCT leaflet You can do it here! or visit www.infantfeeding.info and search for Breastfeeding Out and About.

** The names of some of these items, such as Hooter Hiders, reveal an unfortunate attitude to babies' favourite feeding stations.

FIT TO BUST

The Secret Drinker

(tune: 'I whistle a happy tune' from *The King and I*)[*]

When Mum's in the shopping mall,
and I decide to munch,
we snuggle beneath a shawl,
and no-one knows that I'm having lunch.
When Mum has a plate of chips,
and I feel peckish too,
she opens her hidden zips,
and no-one sees what I love to do.

I am very pleased with the juice she can provide;
always freshly squeezed from the fruit of Mother's pride.

There's nothing to boil or mix,
no teats to sterilise;
I rapidly get my fix —
we're both of us content, feeding-wise!

Even without a shawl, there's usually very little to see. Using some sort of cover may work for a few weeks, but older babies have a disconcerting habit of undocking without warning, often taking the covers with them. This would not have bothered some mothers a century ago.

On the bus the other day a woman with a baby sat
opposite, the baby bawled, and the woman at once
began to unlace herself, exposing a large red udder,
which she swung into the baby's face. The infant,
however, continued to cry and the woman said, 'Come on,

---

[*]   When using the music, note that lines 1–4 and 7–8 are sung to the main theme, lines 5–6 to the third theme.

there's a good boy – if you don't, I shall give it to the gentleman opposite.'

W.N.P. Barbellion, English essayist and diarist (1889–1919) *The Journal of a Disappointed Man* (1919)

Taboo-b

In many Western countries there is a deep-seated taboo against the sight of a breast in a babycare context. The social networking site Facebook regularly removes profile pictures showing breastfeeding, although you can see more flesh in many other profiles. The American midwife Ina May Gaskin has a whole chapter on 'nipplephobia' in her book *Ina May's Guide to Breastfeeding*. She displays the cover of the first edition of *Fit to Bust*, and deplores the fact that this image would probably not be acceptable to an American publisher.*

---

* This edition of *Fit to Bust* is, fortunately, available in the USA from the English publisher, either online or by special order at bookshops.

Vacation lactation

Whenever Tony and I are on holiday – usually camping by the sea – I look out for my nursing pair. We can't go home until we've seen at least one, which I can generally spot at 100 paces. These photos were taken during boat trips to Caldey Island and Skomer Island.

I told one mother how good it was too see her nursing the baby during the rocky trip, although I was sure no one else had noticed. "I was mortified that he asked for it," she replied. "I'd deliberately fed him just before we left!" She was reassured to learn that it was probably comfort rather than food that was needed, and that he knew where to find it.

Coping with complaints

The following song, composed by Janet Russell of the group Sisters Unlimited, is available on the CD *No Bed of Roses* on the Fellside Records label. It has a lovely, catchy tune. On notes accompanying the audiotape, No Limits, made in 1991, Janet says:

9. OUT IN THE OPEN

I wrote this song after the birth of my son Tom, but it had been waiting to be written for four years – since the time when a friend was asked to leave a café in Preston Park, Brighton. The events of the song are true and after the "feed-in", Brighton council passed a bye-law giving nursing mothers the right to feed their children in public on council property.

Breastfeeding baby in the park

Refrain
*Breastfeeding baby in the park,
you'll have to go and do it after dark;
there are parts of you and me
that other people don't want to see –
you can't breastfeed your baby in the park*

*There is a lovely park in Brighton town
with a café where you can go and sit down;
I went to take a rest and drink some orange juice, fresh-pressed,
when my baby's face screwed up into a frown.*

*Well I wasn't exactly looking like Page Three (who needs it?)
as I unhitched my denim dungarees.
The baby soon went quiet, but the staff began to riot
at the sight of this working part of me!*

Refrain

*Well the manageress's face became quite red
as angrily she came to me and said,
"You're a public disgrace, will you please leave this place
and don't come back until your baby's fed!"*

FIT TO BUST

Why is it in the papers every day
that soft-porn on Page Three is still OK?
But if you don't stick them out with a wriggle and a pout
you're told in no uncertain terms, "Put them away!"

Refrain

Well when I thought this it made my anger rise;
I said to myself, "Go out and organise:
what this café is needing is a mother and baby feed-in,
and we'll get rid of some values I despise."

Well the press and local councillors were there,
and the nursing mothers sat in every chair.
Well it really makes me smile, because I took revenge in style,
it was a satisfying moment, fine and rare.

Now there's a bye-law says, "In places selling teas
you can breastfeed your baby when you please.
Brighton cordially invites you to feed the little mites,
and we won't treat you as if you are diseased."

Last refrain
Breastfeeding baby in the park,
you don't have to go and do it after dark;
be it breakfast, tea or lunch, or any time you need to munch,
you've a right to breastfeed baby in the park!

© Janet Russell

HATHOR the COWGODDESS

THE HUMANICUM BREASTFEEDICUS- A LACTATING HUMAN COMFORTABLY BREASTFEEDING IN A PUBLIC SETTING. NOTEWORTHY FOR HER LACK OF ATTIRE AND THE SUCKLING INFANT, THE LARGER HUMANICUM GROUP ACCEPTS HER AS COMPLETELY NORMAL. THIS TYPE OF HUMAN (BREASTFEEDICUS) IS A COMMON SIGHT IN MOST PARTS OF THE WORLD.

FIG. I
HUMANICUM BREASTFEEDICUS PHOTOGRAPHED IN THE WILD OF VONDELPARK, AMSTERDAM. CIRCA 1999

IN THE UNITED STATES SIGHTINGS OF HUMANICUM BREASTFEEDICUS ARE EXTREMELY RARE DUE TO ENCROACHMENT BY HUMANICUM IDIOTUS

© HEATHER CUSHMAN-DOWDEE THE COWGODDESS.COM

Some years ago the following story was posted on a website named 'Breastfeeding UK':

> Back in Jan 94 I had been up to see my parents with DS1
> (darling son) then aged about 10 weeks in my Citroen, it
> was snowing on the way back and my car ground to a halt
> on the A1 (in North Yorkshire) which in those days had no
> emergency phones. I had to walk miles to find someone in
> a cottage who would let me borrow their phone (good job I
> had my sling with me), then miles back, whereupon I imme-
> diately put my starving DS onto the boob. As if by magic a
> policeman appeared to tell me I couldn't stop to feed my
> baby on that road!!!!! I put him right and he went on his
> way, and the car was soon fixed but it took us hours to get
> home then because of the snow. I suspect with a bottle fed
> baby I might well have had no bottles for the supposed
> half-hour trip, but I could just stop and feed DS whenever.
> My mum complained to NY Police about the anti-BF
> constable though, and they did call round and apologise.

Surely the situation is a lot better by now – isn't it?

Protest and protect

In the first half of 2008, growing discontent with the lack of protection for nursing in public in most of the UK resulted in several
supportive newspaper articles. Some cited the National Gallery
incident of 2004, when a breastfeeding mother was asked to move
away from portraits which included 'The Origin of the Milky Way'*.
The same year, Veronika Robinson, author of *The Drinks Are On Me*,
who features in the TV documentary *Extraordinary Breastfeeding*,
started a Downing Street e-petition for legislation to protect the
rights of babies to breastfeed anywhere. Within a couple of weeks,

---

* See Chapter 21 for a cartoon inspired by this painting

9. OUT IN THE OPEN

6,000 people had signed it. Demonstrations in London and elsewhere were organised by Veronika, and Morgan Gallagher who chairs the breastfeeding advocacy organisation Nursing Matters.

These events inspired two songs; the first is named after Morgan's title for the national breastfeeding picnics she arranged that summer. These picnics have become an annual event.

Protect my baby, protect me
(tune: 'It's a long way to Tipperary')

Please protect me, protect my baby, at our breastfeeding time,
for it keeps us both fit and happy, and it should not be a crime.
We ask the nation's leaders injustice to reject;
please protect me, and protect my baby, and show us respect!

The song's first performance on Parliament Square can be viewed on YouTube under the title 'Equality bill protest'. Shortly after we sang it, a BBC reporter filming an interview for News at Six asked a nursing mother in the group to move out of view. How odd that a programme that routinely shows violent behaviour cannot screen an activity which could reduce it! Another mother, on her way home from the demo, was reduced to tears by a commuter's outspoken disapproval when she nursed her baby on the train.

Mothers who are ordered not to feed in a public place could sing this version of the above song:

Respect!

Please respect me, respect my baby, at our breastfeeding time,
for it keeps us both fit and happy, and it should not be a crime.
I'm here because he needs me, so don't call the police;
please respect me and respect my baby, and leave us in peace!

If women are asked to go elsewhere to feed, they could get free advice from the Citizen's Advice Bureau on lodging a formal complaint under the Sex Discrimination Act, or the Equality Act of

Babies have a right to breastfeed anywhere – and a left

2010. This new Act makes it illegal for women to be discriminated against, asked to leave a venue or be treated unfavourably because they're breastfeeding. However, the two clauses that mention breastfeeding refer only to goods and services provided to the mother of a baby under 26 weeks. The Acts do not address a baby's right to be breastfed in any place where he is allowed to go. Scotland alone protects this right.[21]

This song is dedicated to Alison Baum of Best Beginnings, seen above on Table Mountain in South Africa.

On top of the world
(tune: refrain to the song by The Carpenters)

I'm on the top of the world
looking down on my baby,
who is maybe sensing all the joy I feel;
for the love that we've found
keeps us permanently bound,
in a union we can never conceal.

Chapter 10

Going on normally

Breastfeeding beyond weaning

The term 'weaning' here refers to the introduction of solid food, rather than taking the baby off the breast, although these two events may coincide. (The Department of Health's recommendation of six months for exclusive breastfeeding is often interpreted as the limit of any breastfeeding.) Studies comparing humans with other mammals suggest that the natural span of breastfeeding lies between two-and-a-half and seven years. Anthropologist and BF specialist Dr Kathy Dettwyler has written extensively on this subject.[22]

The Notre Dame Psychology Professor Darcia Narvaez, whose research into ancient practices is quoted in the first chapter, identifies six characteristics of child-rearing common to our distant ancestors and still appropriate today. One is breastfeeding, "ideally two to five years, because a child's immune system isn't fully formed until age six, and breastmilk provides its building blocks".[23]

Isn't she a bit old for that now?

What? She's only 30!

Historical references to a recommended (rather than natural) duration show a downward trend, from around three years in the third century BC to just a few months in more recent times. In the past, continued nursing was practically essential for survival beyond infancy. Dr Simon Mays of English Heritage has examined the bones of children found in the deserted mediaeval site of Wharram Percy in Yorkshire. He concludes that they were breastfed for up to two years, and states that this was important for their early survival in a deprived area.[24]

Stopping the flow

During the twentieth century, artificial feeding became a money-spinner, and women were positively discouraged from breastfeeding into the second year. My mother's generation generally stopped at around nine months. Now there is growing evidence that breastfeeding for less than two years is associated with higher risks to maternal and infant health. WHO recommends exclusive breastfeeding for six months, with complementary foods added as nursing continues to two years and beyond.[25] However, at the time of writing, the Department of Health's information is far less clear. For example, the Food Standards Agency advises that breastfeeding may continue to a year 'and beyond', but omits any mention of the risks of early curtailment. Moreover, its advice on milk for babies over one year of age and toddlers ignores the human variety.[26]

In August 2010, a proposal was made to cut government funding of free milk for children. In response, The Times nutritionist Amanda Ursell and Dr Christian Jessen in The Daily Telegraph both stated that toddlers did not need milk, and made no mention of mother's own. If the health service does not acknowledge that breastfeeding is important for at least two years, how will anyone else know?

This next song, about the timespan that children might choose, is dedicated to Ann Sinnott. Her book Breastfeeding Older Children gives fascinating information about the topic from a global perspective, with reports from some of the 2,000 parents in forty-eight countries who responded to her surveys.

10. GOING ON NORMALLY

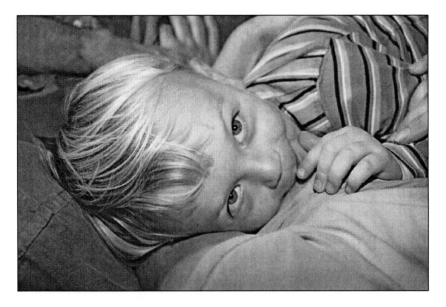

Don't give up yet!
(tune: 'When I'm sixty-four' sung by The Beatles)

When I was younger, before I could bite,
many weeks ago,
you were always ready with a milky meal
every time I made an appeal.
Now that I'm teething, I fear that you might
this fine fare withhold;
but I'll be needing lots of breastfeeding
when I'm one year old.

I can have my breakfast in your bed
and lunch and dinner from your plate, with a drink or three,
and nightcap at ten pm;
but when Granny takes care of me,
I'll have EBM.*

---

* Expressed Breast Milk

As I get older, running around,
tummy bugs will strike;
if you keep on feeding me, or re-lactate,
with your milk I'll self-medicate.
When I fall down, with an ear-splitting sound,
nursing stops my tears;
Mummy, I'm pleading, carry on feeding,
give me two more years.

Every time you nurse me you're developing
my social skills and intelligence;
and my taste buds too;
Milk from cow mummies makes no sense,
I prefer home-brew!

When I start talking, there'll be no disgrace
in making known my needs;
calling out, as on your blouse I land a punch,
"Hurry up and open for lunch!"
Holding each other in loving embrace,
who could ask for more?
Will you still please me, will you still feed me
when I'm nearly four?

Solid evidence

The best time to start babies on food has been hotly debated for centuries. Fifty years ago, parents of my mother's generation were given conflicting advice, ranging from ten weeks to six months. Childcare booklets were full of advertisements for various breast-milk substitutes and weaning foods. The timing of complementary feeding depended on the basis for the advice, either common sense and evidence, or babyfood companies' profits. The same principle holds true today, although company adverts, somewhat limited by legislation, are now far more subtle and sophisticated.

10. GOING ON NORMALLY

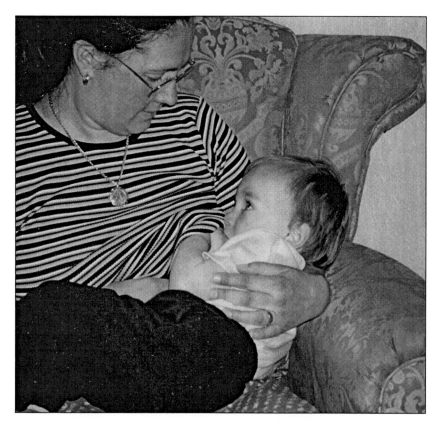

As the ability to take solid food is developmental, like walking and talking, it makes sense to leave the timing to a healthy baby. (Actually, 'solid' is a misnomer for any food given much before six months, as it needs to be liquidised!) This approach is backed up by global research, and has been shown to work well in practice.

Health Visitor Gill Rapley conducted her own video research for a Master's degree, described in the book she wrote with Tracey Murkett entitled *Baby-Led Weaning*. Breastfed babies were given full access to suitable weaning foods from four months of age. Although they showed interest in the food, playing with it and putting it into their mouths, they didn't actually begin to chew and swallow it until they were six months old. This behaviour has been seen in many other babies. One mother who tried this approach, known online as 'Aitch', set up the Baby-Led Weaning website to give more details and share families' personal experiences.

Gill Rapley stresses that BLW is for all babies, not just those who are breastfed. Indeed, some bottle-feeding mothers find that BLW helps to temper their disappointment at not being able to breast-feed, as it restores their babies' dietary control.

The next song is dedicated to Gill and Aitch, and all mothers who enjoy this approach.

Baby-led weaning
(tune: 'Battle Hymn of The Republic' – with
refrain 'Glory, glory, hallelujah')

Refrain
Wean your baby when he's ready;
let the pace be slow and steady.
Dinner-time is easy-peasy
when weaning's baby-led

Nurse your babe exclusively for half a year or more,
getting help immediately if feeding makes you sore.
Doing what comes naturally will help you to ensure
that weaning's baby-led.

Refrain

Flavours in your milk will vary with a healthy diet,
so when baby grabs your lunch, he's more inclined to try it.
Sloppy food's unnecessary, you don't need to buy it
when weaning's baby-led.

Refrain

Let your baby help himself from plate or finger-bowl;
choking's not a problem when you give him full control.

There's no need to hurry it, he'll soon be on a roll
when weaning's baby-led.

   Refrain

Ready, veggie, go!

A few babies seem to benefit from food before six months. William Strong, whose mother Polly consulted me for help when he was twelve weeks old, was an early starter. Every breastfeed was still very painful by eighteen weeks, so after much thought and prayer she began offering him some mashed fruit and vegetables. When he was five months old, she told me in an email:

Alice at six-and-a-half months,
three weeks into weaning

> *Yesterday his carrot and broccoli was too hot, so I was blowing on each spoonful before he ate it. This morning in bed, he obviously thought my milk was a bit warm. He'd have a couple of sucks, then spit out my nipple and start blowing on it, in exactly the same way. Then he'd look at me sideways, and grin!*

O what a lovely pear

When William's brother Thomas was born, Polly again experienced painful feeding, though it had lessened by the time he started taking solids at six months. However, one day when she was nursing him after his lunch of pasta and fruit, he gave her an unexpected bite. She checked his mouth to see if teeth were coming through, and discovered he was still eating a piece of pear!

Polly's amazing commitment to breastfeeding, despite severe pain, is rooted in the Christian faith she shares with her husband Alex. You can read some of her story on my website under 'Polly: a Strong faith',[27] and more details of the problems she faced from her sons' unusual tongue-ties in Chapter 15.

On a boobicle made for two – or three

Simultaneous nursing of children born at different times brings interesting challenges. Doris Connor, shown opposite with the youngest of her eight children, tells a fascinating story. Her problems stemmed from oversupply; what a pity that she had to give up and use artificial milk five times!

> I started feeding my first four babies myself, but had to stop after only a few days or weeks because of various problems. My health visitor could only suggest formula milk, and I didn't know that breastfeeding counsellors existed! However I knew that I HAD to breastfeed, so I set about learning as much as I could. When baby number five came along, I again developed problems, but couldn't see a counsellor because it was the summer holidays. So I gave up, despairing that I would ever be able to breastfeed. When number six was on her way, I wondered if I could bear to try again. However, I came across a poster for a La Leche League (LLL) meeting, and joined my local group.
>
> When Molly was born, she latched on easily, but then hardly ever let go! She fed hourly for her first year, but I coped by carrying her in a sling and co-sleeping. Getting

10. GOING ON NORMALLY

Three's not a crowd

support from my LLL leaders* and finding information
online about others with similar problems, gave me the
courage to carry on. I had not planned to feed beyond a
year, but Molly clearly needed to continue, and by that
time I had become besotted with BF. I became a LLL
leader soon afterwards, so I could help other mothers
experience this wonderful relationship. I was still nursing
Molly when I became pregnant again, and when I saw a
mother tandem feeding at a LLL conference I was inspired
to do the same myself! People warned me that that
continuing to BF during pregnancy would harm my unborn
baby, but they were proved wrong by Gabrielle's birth
weight of 11lb 12oz!

---

* LLL-trained BFCs

Tandem feeding then became a reality, and after the usual problems had resolved, a real joy. The girls became very close, holding hands and stroking each other's hair when nursing together, and were quite happy to nap together when Mummy needed a well-deserved rest. Three years later, Molly weaned herself when I became pregnant again, but Gabrielle continued right through. She got frustrated when the milk supply waned in the later months, but was delighted when Tj was born and it all came flooding back! Molly used to love watching me feed them both, and occasionally asked to nurse too, but mostly it was only two at a time. Gabs is now five, and has just given up feeding. So I'm only nursing Tj now, and may never tandem feed again. I don't know whether I'm relieved or sad about this, but I am very happy that I've been continuously nursing for well over eight years now. *

Role model

After receiving a copy of *Fit to Bust*, Nell McAndrew, glamour model, TV presenter and breastfeeding mother, commented:

As I am still breastfeeding my two-year-old son, I am very pleased to see that Alison Blenkinsop is doing an amazing job of trying to inform more people that to breastfeed is perfectly normal, especially beyond babyhood.

In March 2009, Nell gave an interview to the *Daily Mirror* about breastfeeding Devon, who was then two-and-a-half years old. Her reaction to constant negative comments about this was not to justify herself but to ask, 'Well why not?' She said that no one had ever given her any good reason not to continue.

---

* Adapted with permission from notes on a social network site, May 2010. Doris's ninth baby is due in the summer of 2011!

10. GOING ON NORMALLY

Time to stop?

Some mothers don't want to continue breastfeeding, and appear grateful for reasons or excuses to stop. This may be because continuing beyond the child's first year is seen by many as unnecessary, weird, or even psychologically damaging for children – especially boys. The Channel 4 documentary *Extraordinary Breastfeeding** of 2006 provoked a wide range of opinions both from those interviewed, and from viewers of the programme. The film features Veronika Robinson, editor of *The Mother* magazine, and her daughters, who are shown explaining that breastmilk is even more delicious than mangoes. Veronika points out that children do eventually stop on their own!

> For an unusual view of a closure to breastfeeding, see www.breastfeeding.com for a poem entitled 'Wean Me Gently'.

Even when nursing does come to an end, the supply may continue for a long time. One day, a work colleague asked me whether leakage of milk five years after she'd stopped feeding was normal. I posted this query on an online chat group, and had a number of replies showing that this was common. One BFC said that for several years after weaning she had been able to express some colostrum-like fluid, and she'd just had another try and got something! BFC Dr Wendy Jones then posted this story:

> *One mum told me in an antenatal group many years ago that about six months after she had stopped feeding her previous child, she went to an aquarium, and the sight*

---

* The documentary can be viewed on YouTube.

of the fish coming towards her opening and closing their mouths triggered a let-down! I've heard of barracuda babies, but this made me laugh.

Chapter 11

A child's eye view

Growing up with breastfeeding

I remember sitting on my mother's bed when I was four, looking at cartoons about a cat called Semolina Silkpaws in *Good Housekeeping* while Mum fed Shirley. I also have early memories of two other family friends feeding their babies; the marbled appearance of their bosoms was quite fascinating.

I don't recall any reference to breastfeeding in the children's literature I devoured. Modern books show how babies are made, born, and fed. Some contain lovely images of babies at mother's breast, but a great many show bottle-feeding. Moreover, some animal stories are illustrated in ridiculous ways. One book I came across depicted a family of rabbits going for a walk, with a backpack full of bottles!* Children copy what they see.

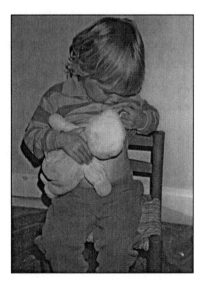

When my sister had her second child, she soothed her painful engorgement with warm compresses in the bath, observed by two-year-old Peter. I bathed him

Honeysuckle Anna and Honey

---

* For another example of a humanised mammal, see my comment on the FurReal Friends Cuddle Chimp in Chapter 20.

later, and noticed him solemnly pressing the sponge to both sides of his chest. Later, after Elizabeth had hand-expressed some colostrum to soften her breasts, he found a glass of what looked like orange juice on her bedside table. He was surprised by the taste!

LC Jane Wallsworth recounts:

> *A mother was telling me that soon after her second child was born, she offered her weaned toddler a feed to relieve her engorgement. He shook his head, but ran off and returned with his plastic beaker and waved it near her chest. She expressed some milk, the toddler sipped curiously, then finished it off and asked for more. After telling me this, perhaps anxious that I would disapprove, she said, "It's OK, isn't it? Won't harm him?" I said, "Oh no – it's got antibodies, immunoglobulins, blah, blah, will help with jealousy…." – all medicalised thinking. The mother laughed and said, "It's sweet, he likes it!"*

Who needs health reasons for using human milk, when the recipients so obviously enjoy it? This gem came from LC Angela Cartwright's breastfed children, composed when they were four and twelve years old.

Booby booby boob
(tune: 'Scooby Doo' theme)

Booby booby boob
Where are you?
I need some milk from you now.
Booby booby boob
I need you,
you make me feel much better.

Statue, Mum?

Some people think that once children can talk, they are too old for breastfeeding. However, vocal requests start young, as Angela recounts:

A good friend of mine is tandem feeding her two-year-old child and eight-month-old baby. In her house what we call 'boobies' has always been called 'mees'. From about five months her baby has made the same sound, 'mees', when wanting to be fed, probably as she has noticed the two-year-old always gets results with this. The baby has Down's Syndrome, and last time she was seen by staff at the child development centre, they were surprised how well she is, and that she is sitting and almost crawling. Mum was delighted to tell them that she can also say a meaningful word!*

When children are able to talk about their nursing experiences, they refer to breasts and milk in the most glowing terms, as in *Extraordinary Breastfeeding*. They don't share women's common concerns about the appearance of their breasts, and may show interest in anything that looks like the real thing (see the previous page).

A nativity story with a difference was posted on the former parenting website Hunnybeez a few years ago.

Went to Abigail's school Christmas concert (no "proper" Nativity this year). Each class did a little something followed by a song or two. Anyway, Ab's class did a Nativity scene, with Ab as Mary (how proud was I?). A few mins into their bit Ab promptly lifted her dress and shoved baby Jesus up it. The script then wandered away from what they'd learnt and went as follows....

---

* Nursing is particularly important for Down's babies; most mothers will need close support to establish and maintain breastfeeding.

Joseph: "What are you doing?"
Mary: "I'm feeding our baby."
Shepherd: "Have you got a bottle up there then?"
Mary: "Don't be silly, he's having milk from my booby."
Joseph: "That's disgusting."
Mary: "No, that baby milk they have in Tesco's is disgusting. My baby's having proper milk."
Shepherd: "What's a booby?"
Mary: "Those sticky out bits ladies have."
Shepherd: "They're not boobies, they're nipples."
Mary: "No they're not, they're boobies."
Joseph: "So why can't Jesus have milk from a bottle then?"
Mary: "Because I haven't got a breast pump with me – you forgot to put it on the donkey."
Shepherd: "Can't you ask the teacher for a bottle to feed Jesus with?"
Mary: "No, because this is the best way to feed Jesus. Anyway bottles haven't been invented yet, and even if they were I've just had a baby, so if you think I'm faffing about round Tesco's to buy baby milk when I make proper milk in my boobies, you can think again."

Hello Dolly

LC Hilary Myers found that her five-year-old granddaughter had a better grip on reality than she did.

> I have one of those dolls that breastfeeds her baby. They come from South America and have press-studs for nipples. The tiny baby doll is attached to the mother by a cord, with a mouth that fixes to the mother's breast. Alisha, who was breastfed for three years, loves to play with it. One day I was out of the room, and on return found that mother and baby were at different ends of the room. "Why is the baby

*not with her mummy?" I asked. "Because it's been naughty,"
was her reply.*

*Before I even thought what I was saying, I responded,
"But it can't be naughty, it's a newborn baby and needs to
be with its Mummy." I continued in the vein of newborns
needing skin-to-skin contact, and how they don't have the
ability to manipulate their caregivers. All the time I could
hear myself getting more passionate, until eventually Alisha
interrupted me. With her hands on her hips and her head
to one side, she said quietly, "Grannie, it's just a game – it
isn't a real baby, you know."*

Larger breastfeeding dolls are now available, as BF advocate Pip
Wheelwright has created a mother and baby pair called Boobie
Buddies. The baby attaches to the mother by hidden magnets, and
the dolls can be used both for play and for teaching purposes.

Ellora with Boobie Buddies in action

Another advocate, Tracey Mulryne, has created Boobee Mammas. She makes various items from socks, including a nursing doll and babies.

These dolls are a welcome replacement for the common-or-garden baby doll, complete with a hole in its mouth for a mini-bottle and dummy!

Nursery Versery for the young at heart

The first rhyme celebrates the work of the UK Association of Milk Banking under its dedicated director Gillian Weaver. The UKAMB website has its own songs to celebrate milk donation!

> ### Two bags full
> ('Baa baa black sheep')
>
> *Nursing mother, have you milk to spare?*
> *Yes sir, yes ma'am, lots to share.*
> *Some for my baby,*
> *and my two-year-old,*
> *and some for the milk bank, worth its weight in gold.*

FIT TO BUST

Golden Delicious
('I had a little nut tree')

I had a little milk tree
which I would often bare,
pressing golden droplets
from a silver pair.

My precious newborn daughter
loved to visit me,
and thrived upon the fruit
of my little milk tree.

11. A CHILD'S EYE VIEW

My goodness
('Jack Horner')

Mum of Jack Horner sat in the corner,
heeding her baby's cry;
she opened her shirt, and gave him a squirt,
and said, "What a good mum am I!"

Joined up drinking
('Rock-a-bye baby')

Rock-a-bye baby under my top,
when he's replete, the feasting will stop,
when he awakes, there's no need to call,
down will come riches under my shawl.

Rock-a-bye baby in the right place,
soothed by my voice, my touch, my embrace;
when you awake, you'll know I'm nearby;
you will feel safe, there's no need to cry.

The next rhyme is dedicated to Mr Mervyn Griffiths, paediatric surgeon and prolific tongue-tie snipper – see Chapter 15.

Divide and conquer
('The grand old Duke of York')

O the grand old Mervyn G
saw thousands of tongue-ties;
he knew that the babies couldn't feed
and he heard their mothers' cries.
So he freed each tight tongue-tip,
taught others how to snip,
and most of their problems disappeared –
dear Merv deserves a prize!

FIT TO BUST

LAM-post[*]
('There was an old woman')

The friend of the woman who lived in a shoe
had only four children – she knew what to do.
She fed every baby herself for three years,
so grand-multiparity gave her no fears!

Fat chance
('Pop goes the weasel')

Half a pint of formula milk,
jars of mince and gravy;
that's the way obesity starts,
pop! goes the baby.

This describes the unfortunate situation in some parts of the UK:

Open for lunch
('Little Miss Muffet')

Little Miss Murphy sat in a café
feeding her baby son.
There came an inspector to give her a lecture,
He said, "Woe are you, you're undone!"

In contrast, the next song celebrates the Breastfeeding etc. (Scotland) Act of 2005.[28]

No snack bar
('Mary had a little lamb')

Morag has two little bairns
with clothes of pink and blue;
and everywhere that Morag goes
the breastfed twins go too.
Now people never harass them,

---

[*] LAM (Lactational Amenorrhoea Method) – see Chapter 12

Two for the price of one

because of Scottish law;
her nurslings don't embarrass them
'cos that's what breasts are for!

I posted the next song in draft form on a breastfeeding supporters' online chatgroup late one night, after a discussion about advice given on strict routines for breastfeeding.

Tickery Quackery Mock
('Hickory Dickory Dock')

These 'experts' should go in the dock,
defending the role of the clock.
Successful lactation
predates its creation;
our verdict is 'Pure poppycock!'

Breastfeeding's a beach

A short while later, BFC Charlotte Thomas responded with this:

A guru, an expert, a doc,
all saying you must watch the clock,
to sleep or to feed
there's really no need,
'cos mother's own instinct just rocks.

Chapter 12

The world of breastfeeding

A global view of culture and practice

Pakistan

In 1976 I moved to Pakistan as a partner with the Church Mission Society. My main role was nursing and midwifery in Pennell Memorial Hospital,* in Bannu. This small town lies near the border of north-west Pakistan in what is now known as Khyber Pakhtunkhwa Province. It's close to areas under tribal rule, and occasionally features in current news of Taliban extremism. I knew it was God's chosen place for me when I discovered that my parents had met there in 1943, during the days of the British Raj. I learned a great deal about life and midwifery in my thirteen years there, and came to love the place and the people, despite many frustrations.

I learned how easy breastfeeding could be when everyone accepted it as normal, and when babies were carried around and fed whenever they wished. It took some time to get used to seeing a small child climb on mother's lap, open her bodice, pull out a breast and suck it like an orange, before running off again. I found it rather unnerving to discuss a woman's medical complaint while her baby fed from one side and played doorbells with the other. Now I realise how normal this is!

I also saw how easy it was for babymilk companies like Nestlé to encourage bottle-feeding. Baby Milk Action has used an image of a Pakistani mother and her twins to show the dangers of unsafe

---

* It is now named Pennell Memorial Christian Hospital

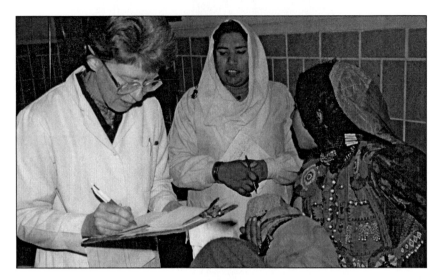

Dr Ruth Coggan OBE and staff nurse with first-time mother and newborn

formula feeding. She was told she wouldn't have enough milk for two. One baby is breastfed and thriving, the other bottle-fed and dying of malnutrition. I have photographs of four-month-old twins showing the same situation in Bannu. The boy was flourishing at 4.5kg (10lb); the girl, who died the next day, weighed 1.5kg (3lb 5oz). You can read more about the dangers of bottle-feeding in Pakistan in Chapter 21.

Other countries

In Gabon, West Africa, the postage and visa stamps bear an image of a breastfeeding mother and baby. When LC Sue Saunders lived there for some years, she found far fewer feeding problems than in her home area of south-east England.

LC Jean Waldman wrote in Treasure Chest in 2000:

> In Norway, women use shells from the beach as nipple
> protectors. They can be boiled, and are breathable, so are

This is how it's meant to be! This portrait is by Nancy Durrell McKenna, whose organisation Safe Hands for Mothers works to save mothers' and babies' lives in developing countries through the production of high-quality educational visuals.

suitable to protect sore nipples from friction and thus aid healing.

Breastfeeding is actively encouraged in the Philippines. This poster in Manila reads: 'Do it with pride – breastfeed your child'.

In Papua New Guinea, the Pidgin for cloth or material is laplap, so a curtain is 'laplap bilong windo'. A bra is 'laplap bilong milkies'.

12. THE WORLD OF BREASTFEEDING

Fit to Bust in Nigeria

Many countries now have good breastfeeding promotional programmes, and lactation consultants are active in dozens of nations worldwide. However, at the time of writing there are very few LCs in Africa (outside South Africa), and only one in Nigeria – Asibi Onyioza Musa. Asibi, who became accredited in 2008, is partnered with LCGB through the International Lactation Consultant Association (ILCA) for support and friendship. LCGB sent Asibi a first edition copy of this book, and I was both astonished and delighted to hear how she was using it.

> *FIT to BUST is on the timetable, where I read out some exciting topic to the expectant mothers during the talk. It has really added life, funs and values to the mothers, staff and the presentation as a whole. More than ten postnatal mothers have collected the book, read it, digested it and come back with testimonies of how it has improved and enlightened their breastfeeding knowledge on a very lighter mood.*

Here are some extracts from an email to Asibi from one of those mothers.

> *The book was definitely a wonderful one. I thank you very much Matron Asibi and the LCGB for exposing mothers like me to this book to enable us learn more and appreciate the usefulness of exclusive feeding for our babies, not just following the crowd because they do it. I have learnt as well that despite the fact that breast milk is food for our babies, it is also used as treatment for various problems. To my surprise, I never knew that outside Nigeria, mothers breast fed up until two years plus. It can't be easy for them I presume. The formula companies are also indeed misleading mothers and ripping them off as well. I give a*

*big KUDOS to the author of this book and say may God
give her the grace and great wisdom to write more books.*

Asibi attended the 2010 ILCA conference in Texas as a sponsored delegate. Her travel costs were paid by LCGB, whose delegates described her as having a heart of gold. She gave them several beautiful Nigerian outfits, and came away with many books donated by lactation specialists. LCGB's website gives more information about Asibi, illustrated by photographs of her at work.

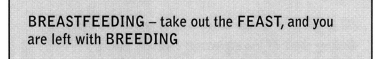

BREASTFEEDING – take out the FEAST, and you are left with BREEDING

In many parts of the world, breastfeeding is not only essential to keep a baby healthy, but also to delay the arrival of the next one.

Lactational Amenorrhoea Method (LAM)

Frequent breastfeeding suppresses ovulation and menstrual periods, and this has been acknowledged by official recognition of LAM as a contraceptive method after global research. The World Health Organisation (WHO) studied more than 4,000 women in seven countries around the world. In the first six months after birth, LAM was equivalent to the protection provided by most temporary contraceptive methods. As three out of four women have no access to barrier or medical contraception, they need natural protection. It's been estimated that breastfeeding prevents more pregnancies worldwide than all other forms of family planning put together. Find out more on the website of World Alliance for Breastfeeding Action.[29]

Lactational amenorrhoea is less common after the first few months in industrialised societies, as well-nourished women may ovulate sooner than those with poorer diets. But frequent breast-feeding can delay fertility for a lot longer than six months.

Many women in north-west Pakistan had husbands working abroad. Keen to get pregnant during their menfolk's short holidays, they would come to the outpatient clinic in Bannu for advice. We often found that they were breastfeeding a two-year-old, and suggested that fertility might return if the child were persuaded to stop. Methods for this included putting bitter substances on the nipple, or tying a length of sewing thread round them.

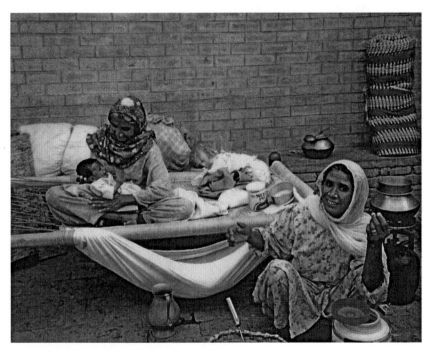

Three generations in North-West Pakistan

Chapter 13

Holy Communication

The spiritual nature of breastfeeding

After I wrote the first edition of this book, I decided not to renew my accreditation as a lactation consultant in 2009. I was becoming more involved with my work as a pastoral assistant and occasional preacher at my parish church, and realised that I could not support new parents as I once could. But my old passions are becoming interwoven with my pastoral work in interesting ways.

The Holy Family

My regular place of retreat, Ladywell Convent[30] in Surrey, has a statue in the grounds showing the Blessed Virgin Mary holding Jesus to her breast. Recent research has highlighted the role of both breastfeeding and a loving upbringing to develop the brain's full potential. My talks and sermons often include a mention of Mary and Joseph's role in making it possible for Jesus to show love to the world.

In Christian art, Mary is often shown with Jesus at her breast; an online search for Maria Lactans will bring up many images. This depiction had multiple layers of meaning for the church, not least the importance of human mother-baby love. However, as breasts began to be viewed as objects of sexual attraction rather than nurturing, many of these paintings disappeared from churches and are now confined to art galleries. But a UK newspaper article in June 2008 stated that the Vatican is calling for the restoration of those images to their rightful place, partly to encourage more women to breastfeed.

Perhaps the Pope could also point out that exclusive breastfeeding is the best natural family planning method!*

The name of the voluntary breastfeeding organisation, La Leche League, was inspired by a shrine in St Augustine, Florida, dedicated to Nuestra Señora de la Leche y Buen Parto. The Spanish words mean "Our Lady of Milk and Happy Childbirth".

The value and significance of breastfeeding is highlighted in the literature and art of many faith traditions. The Bible has a number of references to the nursing pair, a common sight in those times. In Exodus chapter 2, Pharaoh's daughter finds Moses in the bulrushes. His quick-witted sister Miriam suggests finding a

---

* See LAM in chapter 12.

nurse for him – his own mother. In the later book of Ruth, Naomi laid her daughter-in-law Ruth's son in her bosom and became his nurse (Ruth 4:16), maybe to allow his mother to have another baby quickly.

Other religious writings also mention lactation. During my training as a pastoral assistant, I was startled to come across a reference to breastfeeding in the book *The Practice of the Presence of God*. A seventeenth-century monk, Brother Lawrence, says that living in God's presence gives him 'more happiness and gratification than that which a babe enjoys clinging to its nurse's breast.' He describes this joy as 'the breasts of God'.[31]

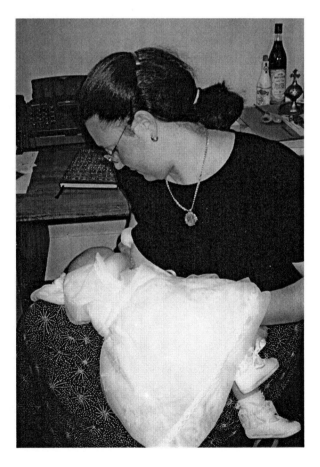

Anna after her
baptism

One verse of the carol 'In the bleak midwinter' mentions 'a breast full of milk'. When I was a child, the line had been bowdlerized to 'a heart full of love'. How good it is to see the original words restored in modern hymnbooks.

This rhyme is not intended as a carol.

> *When Jesus was born, he was dressed*
> *in swaddling clothes, neatly pressed.*
> *Though laid in a manger*
> *he wasn't in danger;*
> *his nourishment came from the breast!*

How love grows

Dr Michel Odent, in his book *The Scientification of Love*, writes about the importance of a loving environment at birth:

> *My vision of the Nativity is inspired by what I have learned from women who have given birth in privacy. It has also been inspired by* Evangelium Jacobi Minori, *the proto-gospel of James, the brother of Jesus. This gospel was saved from oblivion in the middle of the 19th century by the Austrian mystic Jacob Lorber, who wrote* Die Jugend Jesu *(The childhood of Jesus).*

> *According to these texts, Mary had complete privacy when giving birth because Joseph had left her to find a midwife. When he returned with a midwife, Jesus had already been born. It was only when a dazzling light had faded that the midwife realized she was facing an incredible scene: Jesus had already found his mother's breast! Then the midwife said: "Who has ever seen a hardly born baby taking his mother's breast? This is an obvious sign that when he*

*becomes a man, this child will judge the world according to
Love and not according to the Law!"* [32]

Dr Odent points out that very few cultures allow mothers and
babies this sort of freedom; their rituals interfere with early feeding,
and thus increase the risk of aggressiveness. Undisturbed contact,
however, promotes a loving, peaceful environment for raising
children. (See Chapter 7)

Some ancient stories about breastfeeding are hard to swallow.
The following comes from the Christian website Ship of Fools.

Agatha and Azenor: bosom buddies

*St Agatha was tortured to death and her breasts were cut
off, and she was consequently depicted in medieval artwork
as carrying them on a plate, but then things got a bit
confused. Misidentification of these items by the public led
to her becoming the patron saint of bellmakers, bakers and
volcanic eruptions.*

*Which brings us on to Princess Azenor and St Bunoc. When,
in the 5th century, the King of Brest, France, was attacked
by a snake, his daughter Azenor sought the advice of a
nearby (presumably very nearby) wise man. Being a wise
man, he told her to strip and smear her breast with olive
oil and milk, an infallible ruse for alluring snakes. When the
snake left the king and attached himself to her irresistible
bosom, she should cut it off, he told her.*

*The snake fell for the Princess of Brest's booby trap,
and the King was saved. But the ungrateful so-and-so
turned against his daughter, for reasons which to be
frank I haven't quite got to the bottom of, but I think had
something to do with a wicked stepmother and an unex-*

pected pregnancy. He threw her into the sea, shut up in a barrel. There she gave birth to a boy, Budoc, and her bosom was miraculously restored. Thus wondrously equipped she breasted the billows, feeding the baby and steered by angels and saints till after five months they landed in Ireland. Budoc grew up to become a missionary bishop back in Brittany. True story.[33]

Chapter 14

It's never too late

Breastfeeding through the ages

Breastfeeding is possible at any age of childbearing – and even without being pregnant first, through induced lactation. That process has enabled many mothers to feed their adopted children naturally, and enhance bonding. Relactation, even by grandmothers, plays a vital part in saving lives in emergency situations.

Long life milk

A couple of generations ago, British women giving birth over the age of forty were often discouraged from breastfeeding. Many were told that even if they were able to lactate, their milk wouldn't be good enough. But there is no evidence that the milk of older mothers is deficient in any way, and plenty of research to show that human milk is vastly superior to formula. Fortunately, that myth did not put off a sixty-year-old British woman who was recently given fertility treatment, and reported to be breastfeeding her new baby.

There's a story online about another woman who had a baby at the age of sixty-four. Some friends came over to greet the new arrival, and found her alone. When they asked when they could see the baby, she replied, "You'll have to wait until he starts crying." When they asked why, she explained that she'd forgotten where she'd put him.

LC Elvira Henares-Esguerra of the Philippines, who organised the record-breaking 'feed-ins' mentioned in Chapter I, answered an email I'd sent her about the event with this postcript:

*By the way, I am 51 years old and still breastfeeding my
six-year-old child! Not a drop of formula milk was given...
He is healthy, smart, beautiful and very affectionate.*

Dr Elvira is also a Doctor of Medicine, Dermatologist, and
Registered Pharmacist.

Rosebuds and hanging baskets
A teenager comes downstairs wearing a very sheer blouse and
no bra. Her grandmother exclaims, "You can't go out looking
like that!" The girl tells her, "Loosen up, Grams. These are
modern times. You gotta let your rosebuds show!" and out she
goes. The next day she comes down to find her grandmother
with no top on, and just wants to die. She explains that she
has friends coming over, but her grandmother replies, "Loosen
up, Sweetie. If you can show off your rosebuds, then I can
display my hanging baskets."[34]

There are many references on the internet to the nineteenth-
century wet-nurse Judith Waterford, who was still lactating at the age
of eighty-one. She expressed disappointment that she was unable to
nurse more than one baby at a time after her seventy-fifth birthday.

BFC Helen Butler sent me a wonderful account of relactation,
which was apparently little known in thirteenth-century Italy, from *A
Treatise on the Miracles of St Francis*.

*The mother of a small baby died, so her sister nursed
him until she became pregnant again and lost her milk.
The orphan's 80-year-old grandmother, too poor to find
help elsewhere, was bitterly distressed to watch him grow
weaker and weaker. One night she put the baby to her
withered breast to quieten his cries, and tearfully begged
for the help and advice of Blessed Francis. The saint imme-*

diately appeared and said, "Put your breasts in the child's mouth, that the Lord will give you milk in abundance."

The woman did as she was told, and instantly her breasts filled with milk. Many people came to witness this miracle, and saw with amazement that the bent old woman glowed with the warmth of youth. The count of that province doubted the truth of the story. When he arrived to investigate the situation, the wrinkled old woman chased him away by squirting a stream of milk on him.[35]

The Bible's first book, Genesis, reports that Abraham's wife Sarah had a baby in her nineties. She must have breastfed him, as his weaning party is described, and he too lived to a grand old age.

Breastfeeding for this long isn't obligatory. LC Sue Richards sent this story to Treasure Chest:

A woman and a baby were seen by a doctor for the baby's first check-up. The doctor was concerned about the baby's weight and enquired how the baby was being fed. "Breastfed", replied the woman. "Well, strip to your waist," ordered the doctor. He pinched her nipples, then pressed, kneaded and rubbed both breasts for a while in a detailed examination. Motioning her to get dressed, he said, "No wonder this baby is underweight. You don't have any milk." "I know," she said. "I'm his Grandma, but I'm glad I came."

Part Two

Zooming in:
A closer view of the subject

Chapter 15

Don't bottle out

Natural solutions for breastfeeding problems

Let's be realistic – breastfeeding can take some time to get going comfortably. More than three in four UK babies are born with some medical intervention, seven percent are born premature, and some others need immediate specialist care (see the next chapter for more information about their needs). Opiate painkillers, epidurals and surgical deliveries all interfere with the release of hormones that enable spontaneous breastfeeding behaviours. So it's not surprising that one-third of breastfeeding mothers have given up by six weeks, even though most difficulties could have been prevented, or resolved by skilled support. Nine in ten of these women would have liked to continue.[36] So there may be more bottle-feeding by default than from choice!

Read all about it

It's vital to prevent problems, or resolve them early, so that mothers have a real choice to continue breastfeeding. This chapter looks at simple ways to do this. For more complex needs, the online shops of the four main support organisations supply many excellent books and leaflets on preventing or dealing with feeding problems.

However, you won't find some of the highest-selling literature on those sites. If you have a breastfeeding book, take a closer look. What national or international accreditation have the authors gained in breastfeeding education, and what research do they quote?

Our problem is getting a drop out!

Mere personal experience of helping mothers is inadequate for the task of giving reliable, evidence-based information from around the world. Basic midwife, health visitor and medical credentials may be inadequate, because of the many gaps in training. For this reason, the most popular childcare authors, so-called experts and gurus are not necessarily the most reliable.

As well as being a source of trustworthy literature, the voluntary agencies also have wide networks of trained counsellors and peer supporters. The LCGB website carries details of drop-in clinics and support groups, and lactation consultants in private practice. Registered Baby Cafés offer skilled support in a sociable environment. See the contacts section at the end of the book.

15. DON'T BOTTLE OUT

Liquid gold from the treasure chest

When things aren't going well in the first few days, it can be very helpful to hand-express colostrum – the early milk – to give to the baby. I refer to this as 'freshly squeezed' – and it can look just like orange juice! Later on, milk can be pumped to supplement or replace a feed, or give at another time.

Sometimes the breast can become so swollen that the baby cannot attach, and no colostrum or milk can be expressed to give to the baby. This can happen before the milk comes in, especially if the mother has high blood pressure causing oedema (fluid retention). The swelling can affect the breasts, blocking the ducts that carry the milk to the nipple. Such blockages are also common in engorgement, when the milk 'comes in' a few days after birth.

I wrote the next song after learning about 'reverse pressure softening', a way of reducing breast swelling so the baby can attach more easily in the early days. This therapy was developed by American LC Jean Cotterman, and I dedicate the song to her.[37]

Bring back breastfeeding!
(tune: 'My Bonnie lies over the ocean')

Father

My Bonnie cries over our baby,
my Bonnie is very depressed;
the feeds last forever, and maybe
she hasn't enough in her breast.
*   Bring us, bring us, O bring us a bottle of formula;*
*   bring us, bring us a bottle so Bonnie can rest.*

Midwife

I've listened to how you're both feeling,
and well understand your request,
but for comfort your babe is appealing,

so this is what I would suggest.
   Lie back, lie back, O lie back and hold baby skin to skin;
   lie back, lie back, O lie back with babe on your chest.

You see how your baby's relaxing,
he'll sleep while you have a wee rest;
then feeding will not be so taxing,
as long as he's well on the breast.
   Lie back, lie back, and sleep while your baby's in Daddy's arms;
   lie back, lie back, your baby is safe on Dad's chest.

Now baby is looking for luncheon,
but cannot attach, as I'd guessed;
your bosom's too swollen to munch on,
just look at the dents where you've pressed!
   Press back, press back, O press back the swelling
     towards your chest;
   press back, press back, and then you will soften your breast.

And now the colostrum is flowing,
we'll give babe what you've hand-expressed;
this spoonful of nectar is showing
what he will now drink from your breast.
   Bring back, bring back, O bring back your baby
     towards your breast;
   bring back baby – at last, he is feeding with zest!

Father

My Bonnie is now very happy,
and baby's no longer distressed;
there's plenty of proof in his nappy
he's getting his pint of the best.

15. DON'T BOTTLE OUT

All

Bring back, bring back breastfeeding by making it possible;
bring back, bring back, O bring back our babes to the breast!

Nursing bottle with a difference

Another way of dealing with engorgement when a breast pump either isn't available, or doesn't work well, is to use an empty glass bottle. Instructions can be found in a WHO publication which was written for breastfeeding supporters in developing countries.

The top has to be wide enough to accommodate the nipple and areola. The bottle is cleaned, filled with hot water, then emptied; the top is then cooled before being applied to the mother's breast. As the hot air cools, a vacuum is created in the bottle to draw off some milk, which can then be offered to the baby. Eventually the breast becomes soft enough for the baby to feed directly.[38]

When I posted a comment about breastfeeding on a Facebook page in April 2010, I was thrilled to get this message from Eli Murton, whom I'd helped in hospital years earlier:

Alison, you helped me breastfeed my first son when it all
went horribly wrong! I ended up sat with you whilst we
tried using hot bottles to drain my boobs. You were the one
shining light in the whole dire experience. I've since gone
on to have two more, both fully breastfed for over two
years (one still going). Given that no one else had the time
to help me with No.1, I put my BF success in a big way
down to you. Thank you x

Express delivery

When direct feeding isn't possible, an efficient hand or electric breast pump can help mothers keep going for anything from a few days to several months. The next song reminds me of the time when a BFC-midwife told me that pumping for ten minutes each side wasn't as effective as five minutes each side twice over. I suggested this to the next mother I encountered, and she came back with double the volume. (I now suggest pumping only while the milk is flowing, with a maximum time of 20 minutes in total.)

The Breast Pump
(tune: 'The Boyfriend' from the musical)

If women breed, and then breastfeed,
there may be times that they will need
that certain thing called the Breast Pump.
If need to earn means they return
to work, then they may have to learn
self-catering with a breast pump.

Privacy is a necessity, if the milk is to show,
for in order to express it, the oxytocin must flow.
If it's well applied, and not cock-eyed,
and often switched from side to side,
the milk will spring from the breast pump!

Don't bring a bottle

The following song reflects a common scenario where a baby is feeding frequently and taking a lot of milk, but is unsettled and not growing well. Many mothers in this situation are told to supplement with formula or switch to bottle-feeding, in the belief that their (often copious) supply is somehow inadequate.[*] In fact, if the baby is helped to attach more deeply, the milk flows better and is also creamier, so less is needed. Biological nurturing (BN) positions and postures (see Chapter 4) usually result in deeper attachment and more effective feeding. Thus the whole situation can be quickly resolved, as in the fourth verse.

---

[*] This was Doris Connor's experience – see the end of Chapter 10.

15. DON'T BOTTLE OUT

Nursing matters
(tune: 'Oh dear, what can the matter be?')

Refrain:
Oh dear, what can the matter be?
Baby's not getting fatter, he
feeds all day and mum's shattered, she
thinks she will have to give up.

When baby was born he first lay in a stupor
and mum hand-expressed and then pumped like a trooper;
her aim was to make him a three-a-day pooper
with rich EBM in a cup.

But now he is better and feeding directly
and everyone says that he's latched on correctly,
so mum doesn't have any cause to suspect he
does not need a bottle top-up.

Refrain

But baby's positioning needs some correction,
the breast-lumps reveal he can't drain every section,
so milk-fat's reduced, and mum risks an infection –
they need an attachment check-up.

If baby lies prone, then his gape will be wider,
he'll crawl to mum's breast and his actions will guide her,
and then she will have a good feeling inside her
while baby enjoys filling up.

Last refrain
Oh dear, what can the matter be?
Nothing, baby's now fatter, he
feeds well, mum's boobs are flatter, she
now can go onwards and up!

The ties that bind

Decades ago, tongue-tie – a membrane underneath the tongue which can restrict its movement – was routinely divided by frenulotomy (a simple cut into the thin tissue) to allow breastfeeding to continue. Sometime during the second half of the last century, this treatment was largely abandoned in the belief that it wasn't necessary, as babies with ankyloglossia (Greek for fused tongue) could often feed well by bottle. However, a few doctors continued to snip, including Professor Peter Dunn, Emeritus Professor of Paediatrics at Bristol University. We met in 2004 at a neonatal conference where we were both giving presentations. I showed him an LCGB leaflet now named 'Tongue-Tie and Infant Feeding', and he showed me a paper he had written on the subject in 1975. This was about a research project which had used suction apparatus to show that babies with ankyloglossia sucked less strongly than normal controls. Peter has also written a fascinating account of the history of tongue-tie entitled 'Bridled Babies'.[39]

A few months after this encounter, I received a call from Channon Gallichan in Somerset, who was struggling to feed her tongue-tied fourth baby. (Her first was also tongue-tied, but had not been treated.) No treatment was available locally, so I contacted Peter, who referred them to Professor Whitelaw at Southmead Hospital. This resulted in the hospital's first frenulotomy for fifty years, before a fascinated audience. Southmead now has a dedicated service, but Channon still had a fight to get her sixth child treated promptly in 2009.

In recent years the situation has improved, and there are now two dozen hospitals listed on the Baby Friendly website where tongue-tie can be treated by skilled practitioners. Many of these were trained by LC Carolyn Westcott in Southampton, as I was. She and Mr Mervyn Griffiths, Consultant Paediatric Surgeon at Southampton Hospital, have treated thousands of babies. (I did around thirty-five in my last post.) Their research into the condition shows that problematic ties affect around one in twenty babies.[40] Unfortunately, even where

NHS treatment is available, long waiting lists may increase the risk of breastfeeding failure. LCs offering the service privately can be contacted through the LCGB website.

> Tongue-tie does not appear to exist in other mammals, perhaps because of natural selection. I contacted the Jane Goodall Institute to ask about its occurrence in chimpanzees. Jane herself replied that she had never seen it.

Posterior ties

Most cases can be treated simply, with near-instant relief, but a few babies have a more complex condition where the tie is far back and sometimes barely visible (and thus harder to diagnose and treat). Sometimes the baby cannot open his mouth widely, so attachment to the breast is difficult.

My friend Polly Strong's two sons had this kind of tongue restriction; the ties were not diagnosed for several weeks. When William had his first snip at thirteen weeks, he opened wide for the first time! Both babies were treated twice, with obvious improvement but not full resolution, so Polly never enjoyed fully comfortable feeding. The LCGB 'Tongue-Tie and Infant Feeding' leaflet gives more information, and includes photographs of tongue-tied babies before and after treatment. It also refers to NICE (National Institute for Health and Clinical Excellence) guidance on diagnosis and treatment.*[41]

---

* Reports of treatment show that bleeding or infection after treatment is very rare, and easily treated. There is far greater potential for such dangers in a procedure as common as childbirth – cutting the umbilical cord. Research about that appears to be limited to its ideal timing, rather than its fundamental necessity. In fact, cutting the cord is rarely essential; if the cord and placenta are left attached to the baby, they wither and drop off spontaneously after a few days. This practice is called 'lotus birth', and is growing in popularity.

*Ruby shows the
result of her
treatment*

Here's a song to explain how easily the more common condition
can be treated. It's dedicated to Carolyn and Mr Griffiths.

It's a snip!
(tune: 'How do you solve a problem like Maria?' from
The Sound of Music)

*How do you solve a problem like a tongue-tie
when it prevents a babe from feeding well?
Many's the time I've seen a nursing mum cry;
the latch is poor, her nipples are sore, it's hell!*

*How can the baby get a proper mouthful
if the wee tongue is tethered at the tip?
We need to ask the Paed
to watch the baby feed,
the hedge of ignorance we have to clip.*

15. DON'T BOTTLE OUT

So how do you solve a problem like a tongue-tie?
It's very safe and easy, just a snip!

The next song is dedicated to US dentist Brian Palmer, who has
carried out a great deal of research into infant and adult ankyloglossia, finding links from this condition to poor dental health
and obstructive sleep apnoea.[42] It's a plea to the many doctors
who, despite growing evidence of benefit from frenulotomy, remain
unconvinced.

Suspend your disbelief!
(tune: 'Release Me' sung by Engelbert Humperdinck)

Please release my babe's tongue-tie,
the pain of feeding makes me cry;
his tongue's too short to hold my breast,
so release it, we're feeling very stressed.

Please release my child's tongue-tie,
so he can eat his shepherd's pie;
the unchewed pieces make him choke,
so release it, this problem is no joke.

Please release my boy's tongue-tie,
he can't lick ice-creams in July;
his friends poke tongues out when displeased,
so release it, to stop him getting teased.

Please release my son's tongue-tie,
it makes me blush to tell you why;
he wants to kiss his lovely wife,
so release it, to brighten up her life.

Please release my own tongue-tie,
or I'll need dentures by-and-by;

I can't reach back to clean my teeth,
so release it, suspend your disbelief!

Storm in a D-cup

Too many mothers experience mastitis, which usually stems from incomplete milk drainage. GPs often given them antibiotics, but rarely if ever refer them to a breastfeeding specialist, who could sort out the problem and help prevent a recurrence. Prompt attention to clear blockages may also forestall a true infection without recourse to antibiotic therapy, which itself can lead to other problems, such as candida infection (thrush).

I sang the next song at a thrush and mastitis conference organised by pharmacist Wendy Jones PhD, and Magda Sachs PhD, both Breastfeeding Network supporters. Dr Jones and Dr Sachs have produced excellent information leaflets on both topics, which are regularly updated and available on the Breastfeeding Network website.

Thrush and Mastitis
(tune: 'Morning has broken')

Thrush and mastitis, what a disaster!
Baby's unsettled, mother's in pain.
We need to help them find the best treatment
so they'll be feeding gladly again.

Check the position, and the attachment;
snipping a tongue-tie may ease the pain.
When mum expresses, drainage increases,
if it's mastitis, symptoms should wane.

If there's high fever, send for the doctor;
antibiotics may be required.

Resting in bed with plenty of fluids
and analgesia is also desired.

Lack of relief despite good attachment
may indicate that thrush is to blame;
give the right treatment to both mum and baby,
then they'll be happy – that is our aim!

Head start

Some feeding problems seem to arise from distortion of the baby's head during pregnancy and birth, affecting the nerves which supply the mouth and tongue. Many breastfeeding supporters know that cranial treatment from osteopaths or chiropractors can help, but as it is difficult to measure outcomes, some paediatricians dispute its value. However, if they don't offer any alternatives, why should they object to its use?

The following song was inspired by osteopath Tajinder Deoora, author of Healing Through Cranial Osteopathy . I saw how effective this therapy could be when I observed her and others at work at the Osteopathic Centre for Children in London. Since then I have seen many improvements in infant feeding after treatment.

Cradle advice
(tune: 'Edelweiss' from *The Sound of Music*)

Cranial therapy
may help baby with latching;
if his jaw is stiff, or sore,
he'll have trouble attaching.
Bones that are tight are with care put right,
in a gentle action;
colic's eased, Mum is pleased -
both will get satisfaction!

Chapter 16

Special orders

Premature breastfeeding and milk banking

Thanks to modern technology, many premature babies who would once have died are now thriving. But the survival of babies born before twenty-eight weeks of pregnancy depends in large part on milk from their own or another mother. Animal or artificial milk, however highly modified, cannot give the protective factors and growth hormones that babies need for optimum health. Its use can be positively dangerous for those born too soon. Everyone knows the importance of blood donation, but few understand the value of human milk – also known as 'white blood'[43] – which can be banked to save lives.

Milk banking

The first human milk bank opened in 1909 in Vienna. Over the next decades, more banks were set up across Europe and North America, although the advent of AIDS in the 1980s prompted some closures. However, careful screening of potential donors and pasteurisation of their milk has removed infection risks. As evidence of harm from formula feeding mounts up, and more babies survive birth before their seventh womb-month, milk donation is gaining popularity. There are seventeen banks in the UK – six of them in London – and some banks have opened in developing countries such as India. However, there is a huge need for donor schemes to be funded as robustly as blood donation.

When visiting my father in his Berkshire village of Woodcote one day, I met a woman in her fifties who had been born prematurely in Henley. Her mother expressed milk for three months, and sent it to Townlands Hospital on the local bus. Coincidentally, her husband remembers waiting at the same bus stop as a child, to pass on the milk his mother had produced for his baby brother!

Every drop counts

A West London hospital, Queen Charlotte's, was the first in the UK to arrange human milk donation. The milk was given to a set of quadruplets born in St Neot's, a village in Cornwall, in 1935. Their early diet is surely a major reason for their becoming the world's first surviving quads. Four years later, the first milk bank opened at Queen Charlotte's, which has now merged with Chelsea Hospital. The current milk bank's manager, Gillian Weaver, is also one of the founders of UKAMB (United Kingdom Association for Milk Banking). Its website has a link to a YouTube video showing the donation process.

Gillian organised a party at QCCH in May 2010 to celebrate more than seventy years of British milk banking. Specially invited guests included some of the 400 babies a year who benefit from the bank's deposits, as well as Ann Browning, one of the St Neot's quads, who are all still alive and well. Also present were Julie and Jose Carles and their four little girls, who were born in 2006 at Queen Charlotte's and benefited from donor milk as well as their

mother's own. The sisters, who started primary school in the autumn of 2010, are famous for being one of only two living sets of identical quads in the world.

> A mother with identical triplets was telling a friend that this condition happens only once in 64,000 conceptions. Her friend asked in amazement, 'How did you find time for the housework?'

A report of the party can be read on the UKAMB website. Its title, 'Precious Milk for Precious Babies', inspired me to write the following song for a group of donor mothers to perform.

A precious donation!
(tune: 'O what a beautiful morning' from *Oklahoma!*)

When a premature baby is feeding,
and his Mum can't provide all he's needing,
we've plenty to spare, so we're happy to share;
when asked why we do this, we proudly declare:

O what a precious donation, O what delight to express,
poured out as sacred libation, rich overflowing largesse.

For this essence that we are extolling
is the love-food that keeps the world rolling;
it soothes and protects by unrivalled effects,
with flavours that every new baby expects:

O what a precious donation, finer than money can buy,
laying a healthy foundation, free at the points of supply.

We're requesting a big cash injection,
for a national scheme of collection

from just half an ounce to much greater amounts,
recalling this principle, Every Drop Counts:

O what a precious donation, O what a gift to bestow;
let's give a standing ovation to every donor we know:
we want milk banking to grow!

Accompaniment for the donor choir was provided by rock musician Sedleigh, a Queen Charlotte's baby. His moving song *Every Drop Counts* is available on the UKAMB website as a download in response to monetary (rather than mammary) donations.

Savings accounts

Tales of babies saved by donor milk, and of mothers who generously gave it away, can be read on the UKAMB website. One recipient was Rose Petal, whose story appears in *The Politics of Breastfeeding*[44]. She was born with a severe bowel malformation; surgery was unsuccessful, and she was discharged to spend her last days at home. Her mother, unable to nurse her, accepted a friend's offer of breastmilk to keep her comfortable. Against all expectations, the baby began to improve. When more milk was needed, UKAMB organised donations from all over England. Rose Petal's parents are profoundly grateful for the three years that this generosity kept her alive.

Other online stories of babies fed by friends and family after the severe illness or death of their mothers make for heart-warming reading.

Medicine chest

The term Kangaroo Mother Care, mentioned in Chapter 4, originated in Colombia in 1979. It was the only way that some premature babies could survive in an area of limited resources. Since then, this care has been adopted in many countries, because studies show that it is not only much cheaper but also better, in many respects, than standard care. (This usually applies only to babies who aren't ill, and don't need close observation and lots of medical treatment.) It is also better for their mothers. Research by paediatricians such as Nils Bergman in South Africa has shown that any newborn separated from his mother is more stressed than one kept with her.

A premature baby is particularly vulnerable to the stress of life outside the womb. In KMC, he can be nurtured in the next best place, his mother's chest. Body temperature, heart rate, breathing and oxygen levels quickly stabilise in this natural environment. The baby rarely cries, so energy is conserved; his mother's familiar sounds and scent keep him calm, helping him to adapt to the world. For the mother, the infant's presence can be greatly soothing, enabling her to feel an integral and vital part of his care. Because of the hormones released by contact with her baby, her milk let-down reflex and supply can also be enhanced. (This is particularly important when direct breastfeeding isn't yet possible, and milk has to be expressed.)

Babies cared for in this way tend to have shorter hospital stays than those kept in an incubator. They also start breastfeeding sooner and continue for longer. Once the need for skin contact has lessened, babies can continue to be carried around in slings in 'attachment parenting' style.[45]

Wendy had an emergency caesarean delivery at nearly thirty-one weeks for severe pre-eclampsia (a condition which includes high blood pressure). They both made a full recovery. Benjamin started school in the autumn of 2010, and was placed in the top set for everything, which shows that premature babies can do very well. His prowess may also have something to do with ongoing night feeding!

'Miracle' baby

In the autumn of 2010, media accounts began to appear of a mother in Australia, Kate Ogg, who had given birth in March to twins born at twenty-seven weeks. Little Emily was transferred to intensive care, but Jamie, who weighed around 2lb (1kg), could not be resuscitated.

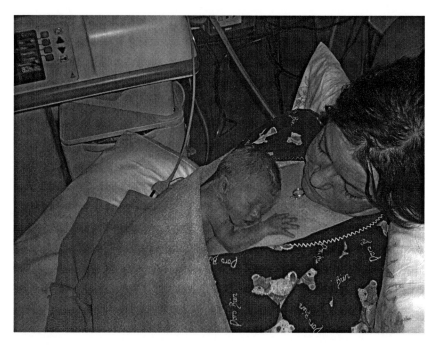

Benjamin, 36 hours after being born ten weeks early, snoozes on his mother Wendy's chest

The doctor gave him to Kate and her husband David for their last farewells. Video footage shows Jamie lifeless under a blanket on his mother's chest, but then responding to caresses and drops of breastmilk. Two hours of KMC had saved Jamie's life! The family is also shown five months later, with both twins fully recovered.[46] A newspaper report is available on the Kangaroo Mother Care website, along with Nils and Jill Bergman's comments.

Jill's recent book *Hold Your Prem* describes in everyday language the key concepts of KMC. Its aim is to empower parents to become central to the paediatric team responsible for their baby's care. Who knows how many other babies could be saved in this way? Maybe our way of caring for babies needs to come full circle.

16. SPECIAL ORDERS

A Short History of Medicine:
"Oh Doctor, I have this terrible pain!"

2000 BC   "Here, eat this root."

AD 1000   "That root is heathen. Say this prayer."

AD 1850   "That prayer is superstition. Drink this potion."

AD 1940   "That potion is snake oil. Swallow this pill."

AD 1985   "That pill is ineffective. Take this antibiotic."

AD 2000   "That antibiotic is artificial. Here, eat this root".[47]

A Short History of Babycare:
"Oh Doctor, how should I look after my baby?"

2000 BC   "Just carry it next to your skin. Breastfeed it whenever it is hungry."

AD 1660   "Breastfeeding is undignified. Hand it over to a wet-nurse."

AD 1850   "Wet-nurses are low class and have an undesirable influence on the child. Get a good experienced nanny to give it cow's milk."

AD 1930   "Cow's milk is unsuitable for babies. It must be bottle-fed on a special infant formula."

AD 1950   "Bottle-feeding at all hours is bad for the baby. Follow a strict routine, let it sleep in its own room and ignore it when it cries at other times."

AD 2000   "Bottle-feeding is unsuitable, a strict time-table is nonsense, babies don't like being alone, and crying is stressful. Just carry it next to your skin. Breastfeed it whenever it is hungry."[48]

The 'Skincubator'
21st century bespoke care for the premature infant

Excitement is growing about this recently discovered item of equipment designed for non-ventilated infants. The Skincubator® comes fully assembled, needs no electrical wiring, and can be easily transported. It is soft and warm to the touch, with highly advanced thermoregulation controlled by its occupant, providing an environment as near as possible to the former residence. The surface is pre-treated with a protective layer of beneficial bacteria, while harmful pathogens are easily removed by plain water. The Skincubator provides individualised aromatherapy, with attachments for positive touch therapy and gentle massage during the infant's wakeful periods. Background auditory effects are enhanced by soothing sounds triggered by a call system. An area of extra cushioning provides comfort without obstruction of the airway, when the head is placed correctly between its contours.

Nutrition is freshly prepared by inbuilt sensors, and carefully formulated to meet the infant's exact requirements. It may be delivered direct by oral control, or extracted frequently and given by other means, with any surplus stored elsewhere for later use. This food contains anti-infective agents, which alter daily to meet new potential hazards, and provides subtle variations in flavour to promote gradual progression to a culturally appropriate diet. A built-in alarm system alerts the caregiver instantly to any untoward change in the infant's condition or behaviour.

Some carers are puzzled at the delay by Western hospitals to accept and use this technogical marvel, which has been used extensively in the developing world for years. The Skincubator has in fact been a standard fixture in all premature baby units for years, though its use has been very limited; until recent decades, it was kept away from the unit outside visiting times. Nowadays, it may be removed while staff attempt to replicate its provision with less reliable equipment, which is very expensive to purchase and maintain. In contrast, the Skincubator costs the hospital very little to install and keep in service, the only requirements being a padded adjustable surface, free access to high-quality food and fluids, and a commitment from hospital staff to encourage its use.

16. SPECIAL ORDERS

KMC is still not routinely practised in many UK neonatal and maternity units; incubators and 'hot cots' are commonly used. Just before the 'miracle baby' story came out, a BFC known as Analytical Armadillo had written on her blog about the possibility that a piece of technology costing £30,000 might deliver less effective care than a parent. After Jamie's story broke, she began to mobilise others to call for incubators to be replaced, where possible, by 'skincubators' – a term coined by midwife Helena Bull during online discussions. See opposite for a development of this idea.

It seems absurd that funding for expensive equipment, such as overhead or under-the-mattress heaters, seems so much easier to obtain than money for parent-friendly wards, which might greatly reduce the need for such high-tech items. It is also scandalous that specialised 'premature' babymilk is often given higher priority than human milk. My ideal ward would have plenty of space for reclining chairs or beds for parents to carry out KMC, with a cot or incubator available for the baby's use when Mum or Dad isn't around. The ward would be staffed by experts in preterm nutrition of the human variety. Then we would not hear this plaintive cry.

Where is Mum?
(Tune: 'Where is Love?' from *Oliver!*)

Where is Mum? To a strange new world I've come;
lying lonely here in helpless fear,
unable to keep dumb.

Where is she whom I long to hear and see?
Will I ever know the milky flow
that's meant for only me?

Once my life was peaceful night,
now it's often harshly bright,
full of jarring sounds to hurt my ears,
raise my fears, bring my tears;

FIT TO BUST

where, where is Mum?

In her bosom I could hide,
comforted each time I cried,
close encircled by a loving arm,
quiet and warm, safe from harm;
where, where is Mum?

Chapter 17

Cheerleaders

The role of breastfeeding supporters

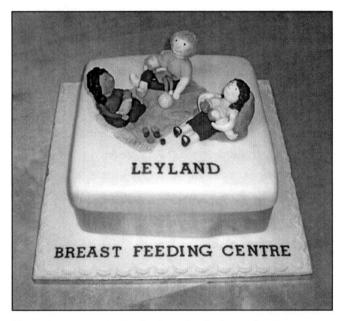

This cake was made for the launch of a breastfeeding group run by Breastfeeding Network Supporters and health visitors in Preston in 2004

UK support organisations

The four voluntary organisations train breastfeeding counsellors and peer supporters, and provide a range of informative leaflets and literature on their websites.

La Leche League* was born in Illinois, USA in 1956, and soon spread to the UK and other countries. It promotes mothering skills as well as natural feeding. The National Childbirth Trust began as an association to promote natural childbirth in the same year. It now helps parents through educational programmes and support groups for matters related to pregnancy, birth, babycare and infant feeding.** The Association of Breastfeeding Mothers was founded in 1979 to focus on support for nursing mothers. The Breastfeeding Network, which broke away from another group to ensure independence from commercial influence, was formed in 1997.

All four groups are represented in Lactation Consultants of Great Britain, and have dedicated websites. Contact details are given at the end of the book.

La Leche League has members in sixty-eight countries, with many groups in the UK. The following song marks the launch of the international magazine *Breastfeeding Today* in the spring of 2010, and celebrates five decades of mother-to-mother help. You can see performances on YouTube by two LLL groups in Kent and the Isle of Man, with an introduction by an excited toddler.

> **La Leche League the beautiful!**
> (tune: 'America the beautiful')
>
> *For fifty years La Leche League*
> *has grown in many lands,*
> *and nature's way to nurture babes*
> *the world now understands.*
> *La Leche League helps mothers feed*
> *their children at their breast,*

---

* See Chapter 13 for the history of its name.

** NCT also speaks out on issues such as poor NHS postnatal care, the impact of child benefit cuts, and the exam question scandal of 2010 mentioned in Chapter 20.

17. CHEERLEADERS

so families may grow in love,
with true well-being blessed!

Peer supporters

This term has been given to women who support other mothers as 'breastfeeding allies' in a reciprocal relationship. It may be a voluntary or paid role, and is similar to that of the doula,* with more emphasis on empathy and encouragement than professional expertise. In an MSc thesis on Peer Support, LC Marilyn Rogers explains that the art of breastfeeding has been lost in many families and societies, and in some areas generations of bottle-feeding have largely obliterated an appreciation of its importance. For this reason, peer supporters are especially important in areas of social deprivation, and they are now commissioned by some Strategic Health Authorities in maternity and childcare services. Accredited breastfeeding educators are in charge of peer support programmes run by the voluntary organisations, but at present not all training and subsequent activity is well regulated.

An example of a peer support programme in an area where bottle-feeding has been the norm for several generations is Little Angels in Darwen, Lancashire. This is a Community Interest Company created to make breastfeeding fashionable as well as providing evidence-based information. It employs peer supporters drawn from the local community, and is involved in various campaigns, such as Be A Star. This campaign, launched by Lancashire Primary Care Trust in early 2008, helped to achieve a thirteen percent increase in breastfeeding initiation over the first six months, against a target of two percent. Be A Star deliberately broke with the usual mother-gazing-at-baby imagery, and has been successfully extended to many other areas since.

One campaign leads to another. Michelle Atkin, former director of Little Angels, reported:

---

* See Chapter 4

Photography by Andy Farrington; Creative Design by The Hub

17. CHEERLEADERS

Little Angels decided to use the theme of Be A Star to promote 'Stars in Town' in Accrington during National Breastfeeding Awareness Week in May 2008. The local Be A Star girl was there to offer information on breastfeeding, and we also had balloons, stickers and badges to give out. A small girl of about four approached the stall, and with her mother's encouragement gave a full rendition of 'Miss Polly Had a Dolly'. One of the Little Angels, Clare, said that it was lovely and gave her a sticker. It was only later that Clare realised the mother had thought that 'Stars in Town' was a chance to audition for the TV show, The X Factor. So her daughter had sung her little heart out and gone away with a sticker to promote breastfeeding!

Baby Friendly Initiative

The Unicef Baby Friendly Hospital Initiative has made a great difference to breastfeeding support worldwide. Research shows that where the Ten Steps to Successful Breastfeeding are followed, initiation rates increase. I wrote this song for Breastfeeding Awareness Week in 2007, and dedicate it to all who work with UK BFI. Bracketed numbers refer to the BFI *Ten Steps to Successful Breastfeeding*.[49]

We all love breastfeeding!
(tune: 'Yellow Submarine', sung by The Beatles)

Refrain
We all love feeding babies at the breast,
babies at the breast,
babies at the breast;
we all love feeding babies at the breast,
babies at the breast,
babies at the breast.

In the place where we give birth
there's a Baby Friendly policy (1) ,
and full training for the staff
so that mums can feed naturally (2).

So throughout the pregnancy
we'll discover how lactation works,
how from problems to be free,
all the benefits and all the perks (3).

Refrain

When our little ones are born
they'll relax with us, skin to skin,
and we'll hold them close and warm
for an hour until they're tucking in (4).

Then we'll keep them by the bed (7)
and give no dummy (9) or a bottle feed (6),
every meal is baby-led (8),
but our milk's expressed if there is need (5).

Refrain

We can all have bosom friends
and a counsellor to call upon,
Baby Cafés to attend,
for encouragement to carry on (10).

Refrain

The Baby Friendly Initiative website lists all hospitals with their current status. You can use a template letter to ask your local hospital about getting accredited. The following song is dedicated to Baby Friendly hospitals, and is a challenge to all the others to follow their lead.

17. CHEERLEADERS

Baby's first picnic
(tune: 'Teddy Bears' Picnic')

If you go down to the wards today
you're in for a big surprise:
a brand-new policy's on display,
and hushed are the infant cries.
For mums' and babies' clothes have been shed,
they're skin to skin together in bed,
for that's the way the babies can freely breastfeed.

Feeding time for girls and boys;
their mums are learning ploys
for helping their little ones attach,
so that everyone enjoys
a satisfying meal and comfy latch.
If the babe won't take the breast,
colostrum's hand-expressed and given without delay;
there's far less jaundice, weight loss is minimal,
mothers are empowered,
and very soon they'll be on their way.

If every hospital in the land
adopted this policy,
then feeding problems would lessen, and
how happy we all should be!
The mums and babes would all be more healthy,
hospitals would then be more wealthy;
let's ensure that babies can freely breastfeed.

A USA Breastfeeding Awareness drive in 2005 used some eye-catching posters. They show pairs of otoscopes, dandelions, and bowls of ice cream with a cherry on top, with respective messages that breastfeeding may reduce the risk of ear infections, respiratory illnesses and obesity.

International Board Certified Lactation Consultants

A lactation consultant is an expert in the fields of human lactation and breastfeeding. An LC may have a medical, nursing or midwifery qualification, or accreditation as a BFC with a voluntary organisation. Naturally, there are many more women than men in most countries. Certification is gained through individualised training pathways and an international exam, with five-yearly recertification.[50] Many countries have their own national group, such as Lactation Consultants of Great Britain.

The term "lactation consultant" is still an unfamiliar term. In response to a letter I wrote to *The Times* in August 2006 about breastmilk being suitable for vegans, a reader asked, "Is a 'lactation consultant' what I used to know on the farm in my youth as a milkmaid?" Some unqualified feeding advisers describe themselves as consultants in breastfeeding or lactation, but only fully accredited IBCLCs can be trusted to deliver all the goods!

The following song celebrates the work of many LCs all over the world who set high standards of care in maternity hospitals. The story is not to be taken too seriously!

All part of the service – a week in the life of a lactation consultant
(tune: 'The Gasman Cometh' sung by Flanders and Swann)

'Twas on the Monday morning I received a frantic call;
a newborn babe was whimpering, and wouldn't feed at all.

17. CHEERLEADERS

We put the baby skin to skin so he'd no longer whinge,
his mum expressed colostrum and we gave it by syringe.

   Refrain
   For it's part of the service IBCLCs provide.

'Twas on the Tuesday morning that I visited the pair,
the infant wasn't feeding yet, and mum was in despair;
we stripped him of his cardigan and baby-suit and vest,
and in her arms he wakened and began to take the breast.

   Refrain

'Twas on the Wednesday morning that the milk was coming in,
the breasts were red and lumpy with a tense and shiny skin;
I showed her how to soften them, to help the baby latch,
and soon a lot of milk was disappearing down the hatch.

   Refrain

On Thursday, babe was jaundiced and examined by the paeds;
they ordered phototherapy and supplementary feeds.
I brought the humilactor out, and helped to set it up,
and showed her how to pump her milk and give it in a cup.

   Refrain

'Twas on the Friday morning babe began to feed and feed,
the nipples started getting sore, and then began to bleed.
I helped her with positioning, to minimise the pain,
and by the evening she was nursing easily again.

   Refrain

'Twas on the Saturday morning mum and baby were discharged;
but soon a wedge of breast was red and hot and quite enlarged.
I told her if she drained it well, then it would soon subside,
and she mightn't need the tablets that the doctor had supplied.

Refrain

(tune to second part of verse)
On Sunday I went off to church, my worries to dispel,
and when I rang on Monday, everything was going well!

LACTATION CONSULTANTS *of* GREAT BRITAIN

LCGB is a membership organisation for LCs and supportive associates. Members aim to raise awareness of the need for both breastfeeding expertise and general support in the health sector and their local communities. It also supports an LC in Nigeria, Asibi Onyioza.[*]

The website homepage greets visitors thus:

> *Lactation consultants have all passed a test*
> *to help mothers nourish their babes at the breast.*
> *So read all about us, and then you'll be free*
> *to contact or join us at LCGB.*

Getting breastfeeding off to a flying start

Australian LC Sue Cox was one of the very first to qualify in 1985, and has produced several books and videos. One of her particular interests is the protection of newborns' feeding instincts. When she spoke at an LCGB conference in 2007 about skin-to-skin contact, she described how the breasts and nipples darken in pregnancy to

---

[*] See Chapter 12

allow babies to spot them. We can imagine how a newborn could also follow the linea nigra, the dark line on the abdomen, as a flight path to either of the twin terminals.[*]

This concept could be expanded in teaching sessions, with a mention of checking the nappy for exhaust emissions. Parents could then be informed that BF is a great way to keep babies comfortable while taking off and landing, as the swallowing helps equalise the air pressure in their ears. See also the story in Chapter 8 about the gallant pilot and the nursing mother.

For budding lactation consultants

This was composed for LCGB's insert in the programme of a national breastfeeding conference.

> *Consultants in lactation are few and far between;*
> *we're giving information, so if you're very keen*
> *on further education to gain qualification,*
> *you'll learn the sum of how to become*
> *an IBCLC Queen![**]*

Here's some advice for those preparing to take the IBLCE exam.

> *As into your head you are trying to cram*
> *every fact and statistic to pass the exam,*
> *I send you this message to warm and inspire you,*
> *to calm, for a moment, the passions that fire you:*
> *it's people like you who enable this image – [see over]*
> *two satisfied parents, with breast-nurtured lamb!*

---

[*] This is part of the infant's ability to find the breast, as detailed in a 'Scientific Overview of Breast Crawl' available online.

[**] LC Kings also exist.

FIT TO BUST

Chapter 18

A handy toolchest

Resources for breastfeeding specialists

Breastfeeding preparation classes should not be like teacher-led school lessons; they can be much more fun!

P   Play with sock breasts and juice-bottle-top baby mouths

A   Aid recall of important information with word play

R   Raise energy levels and help groups to have fun

T   Tell jokes and funny stories

Y   Yummy-up sessions with suggestive biscuits

T   Try out new ideas to get your message across

I   Increase everyone's understanding of babyfood industry tactics

M   Make your own nappies to show the five days of feeding

E   Encourage the celebration of breastfeeding

S   Support Baby Milk Action by using *Fit to Bust*

Throughout this book you can find all the above ideas to make breastfeeding promotion enjoyable, as well as my Latch Key, cartoons (if credited to their creators), and songs suitable for community singing. They are all part of my resource kit, the 'breastfeeding enabler's toolchest'.

American LC Linda Smith has a wonderful collection of games and activities in her book *Coach's Notebook: Games and Strategies for Lactation Education*. In one, she asks participants to suck a small sweet while holding their nose, to explain why nipple shields can affect the taste of breastmilk. Mothers are also asked to make a list of everything they drank in the last twenty-four hours, to show how normal frequent drinking is!

Here are some activities others have tried.

- Get mothers to stand in a circle and massage the shoulder-blades of the woman in front, so they can experience the relaxing effect of oxytocin release.

- Demonstrate the need for a good let-down to maximise milk fat release, by using a sponge to soak up a mixture of food-grade oil and water. Show how the water will drip out on its own, but the oil remains in the sponge until it is squeezed.

- Offer refreshments with a choice of shop-bought biscuits and homemade cakes. Participants will quickly see which are more popular, and realise the implication!

Here's another idea to serve with the drinks.

SUGGESTIVE BISCUITS

Ingredients:

Digestive biscuits, or any small round biscuits — mini ratafia-type are a good colour and shape, being domed

Thin icing coloured pinky-brown, or a tube of icing in a suitable colour (for the areola)

Firmer icing coloured red or dark brown, or half a cherry, or a chocolate chip (for the nipple)

Instructions:

Decorate each biscuit with a circle of light icing, with a dollop of darker icing or a cherry in the centre, or add a squeeze of icing and stick the 'nipple' on.

Community singing

There are many impediments to feeding soon after birth; this song may help mothers remember how to deal with them. It is dedicated to my former job-share partner and LC Kim McHarg, whose encouragement and support kept me going as Infant Feeding Adviser for five years. The song works well with the leader singing the middle line about the proposed intervention, and everyone else joining in the lines either side.

Off the wall
(tune: 'Ten green bottles')

Ten new babies trying to take the breast,
(repeat for first verse only)
and if one new baby in labour was distressed
there'll be nine new babies trying to take the breast.

Nine new babies trying to take the breast,
and if one new baby from pethidine's depressed
there'll be eight new babies trying to take the breast.

Eight new babies trying to take the breast,
and if one new babe's head by forceps was compressed
there'll be seven new babies trying to take the breast.

FIT TO BUST

Seven new babies trying to take the breast,
and if one new baby remains completely dressed
there'll be six new babies trying to take the breast.

Six new babies trying to take the breast,
and if one new baby's removed to have a test
there'll be five new babies trying to take the breast.

Five new babies trying to take the breast,
and if one new baby from light and noise is stressed,
there'll be four new babies trying to take the breast.

Four new babies trying to take the breast,
and if one new baby's too far from mother's chest
there'll be three new babies trying to take the breast.

Three new babies trying to take the breast,
and if one new baby is tongue-tied – yes, you've guessed,
there'll be just two babies feeding at the breast.

Two new babies feeding at the breast,
but if two more babies are stripped to just a vest
there'll be four new babies feeding at the breast.

Four new babies feeding at the breast,
and if two more babies are left with mum to rest
there'll be six new babies feeding at the breast.

Six new babies feeding at the breast,
and if two more babies to mother's skin are pressed
there'll be eight new babies feeding at the breast.

Eight new babies feeding at the breast,
and if two more babies get milk that's hand-expressed,
then the ten new babies with pleasure will be blessed!

Knit 2 together

Dr Michel Odent, author of several books on birth and breastfeeding, states that a midwife quietly knitting in the corner of the room encourages natural birth, as this activity lowers everyone's stress hormones. But what should midwives knit?

One appropriate item would be a breast! BFC Lorna Hartwell, creator of an all-in-one knitting pattern, says:

> My rationale for breast models is this. We shouldn't need them, but given the lack of familiarity with breasts and breastfeeding in this society, a visual aid for demonstrations is necessary as it not easy to use the real thing. Even when a mother is actually feeding her baby, in order to be 'hands off' effectively, it is very useful to be able to show her certain points on a model breast.
>
> I considered:
>
> • Wooden breasts: although beautiful, the texture is hard
>
> • 'Gazza' breasts: perceived as a joke and/or sexual
>
> • Felt material: soft, warm and homely, probably just as good but would need more instructions and materials
>
> • Knitted: soft, homely, warm, very cheap, motherly, infinite number of colours available, can be made with scraps of wool. It is easy to knit a protractile nipple and a flat one, and to vary the size of the areola as well as the breast. This helps to make the point that these differences are often utterly irrelevant to breastfeeding.

Viral yarns

Another pattern created by LC Carolyn Westcott, to make in two parts, can be found on the LCGB shop page. It attracted a great many visitors to the site after the BBC ran a story about woolly breasts in 2007.[51]

LC Kate McFadden, then Infant Feeding Advisor at Liverpool Women's Hospital, explains:

> The knitted breast project started when we needed a large stock of model breasts to teach women about feeding and expressing milk. They can cost £35 each, so when someone in my team gave me a knitting pattern I asked my mother to make some for us. She brought them down on the plane each time she visited from Scotland. Mum wondered how she would explain them if they showed up on the airport security cameras!
>
> I also started knitting breasts, and gave them to the feeding advisors. We started to carry them around with dolls to teach a 'hands-off' technique (ie helping mothers without touching their breasts or babies). One of the Sure Start midwives got involved, and some of the mothers started knitting too. Four generations in one family were supporting this project.
>
> This story was picked up by the Liverpool Echo in February 2007, and passed to the BBC; the Corporation's website had 100,000 hits in one day. The BBC followed up the next day with the heading: 'Woolly breasts go global', with a link to the pattern on the LCGB website.
>
> Several interviews and articles later, knitting websites and magazines in the UK and abroad (including Vogue Knitting in the USA) began to carry the story. Woolly

breasts started flooding in, along with the women's
own childbirth stories. Now all the community midwives,
hospital midwives and neonatal unit staff have their own.

Kate's team won first prize for this project in the British Journal of Midwifery 'Innovator of the Year' award in 2007.

Knitworking

Returning from a holiday in the West Country in the summer of 2010, my sister Mary and I stopped at a church in Cheddar for a look round. As we admired a display of tiny garments made by Mothers' Union members for premature babies, a familiar round object caught my eye. Alongside it was a story from the BBC in May 2010 entitled 'Knitted breasts help mothers', accompanied by the following photograph.[52]

Louise Stickland (Infant Feeding Specialist), Shirley Gibbs (Mothers' Union), Julie Scrancher (Infant Feeding Specialist)

LC Louise Stickland, an Infant Feeding Specialist in Somerset, had heard that the MU were making baby clothes, and commissioned them to provide 150 breasts for local maternity units. When Mary and I called on LC Hilary Myers in Frome later that day, we learned that the suggestion was originally hers, using the LCGB pattern. Louise told me the following autumn that over 300 breasts were being used routinely by health visitors and peer supporters to show mothers how to express their milk by hand.

A quilting club did a bit of 'reclaiming their breasts' in 2010. They served a platter of boobie cup cakes to fellow members as a fundraiser for a breast health charity. The plate had a centrepiece of knitted breasts made by another member for the local LLL group. One 75-year-old member pinned a pair of knitted breasts to her chest and adorned them with the tassels the group was making for their quilting creations. An official who popped into the church hall was a little embarrassed, but the lady was unabashed!

Replacement breasts

I'm used to getting requests for the breast pattern, but was surprised to receive this email in January 2010:

> *Will you please send the pattern for a knitted breast? My great-grandmother has had to have a double mastectomy and I would love to knit her a pair.*

I later learned that this is a serious issue – prosthetic breasts are not always comfortable, and very expensive in countries without free healthcare like the UK. An internet search recently led me to a group based in Maine, USA, which offers 'Knitted Knockers' free to breast cancer survivors. What a great idea!

18. A HANDY TOOLCHEST

Hats off (and on) to breastfeeding

See inside the front cover for a photo of my godson, Thomas Strong, modelling a Fit to Bust hat. The pattern was created by Women's Institute member Cath Hall of Anna Valley, Andover, and is available on my website. Cath is a great knitter, and we first became acquainted when she posted me a package of breasts for LCGB. I later spoke to her Women's Institute about my work, and composed a song for the occasion to the tune of 'Jerusalem'; see the end of the book.

An American couple, Rachel and Joel Green, have created a 'Boobie Beanie' baby hat, which makes it very clear how their baby Ezra is being fed. Those who object to public breastfeeding may have to look twice to check what is actually on view.

Putting a sock in it

I made this breast during a month-long International Breastfeeding Practice and Policy Course at the Institute of Child Health, London, in 1998. At the time, I was based at Kingston Hospital in Surrey. Dr Felicity Savage-King, who has years of experience in helping mothers with breastfeeding in developing countries, showed participants how to make a sock breast and a doll out of two towels. She offered prizes for the best breast and doll. My creation, accompanied by a baby's mouth made from a juice-bottle top and balloon, won a WHO video showing breastfeeding promotion in Kingston Hospital – Jamaica.

An article I wrote about this resource, entitled 'Sock it to me: using a breast model to enable women to establish lactation' is included in the book *Midwifery: Best Practice 2*.[53]

Travel socks

In the spring of 2010 I had an email from LC Debi Faix, a nurse in a Neonatal Intensive Care Unit in New Jersey, wanting information about making a sock breast. Here's some of the correspondence:

18. A HANDY TOOLCHEST

Demonstrating the use of the breast to Dr Gillian Burton (former CMS mission partner in Pakistan) at a Baby Friendly Initiative conference

Debi: Although I am frustrated by the lack of support our hospital gives for breast feeding, I am encouraged by our Neonatologist's interest and commitment that our entire population in the NICU should be breast feeding. The instructions for the sock breast would be a great educational tool. I think I must name my breast model Ali after you :)

Alison: Many thanks for your encouragement, Debi. It is thrilling to be able to have a positive impact on people from a distance. You could name the sock breast Ali Booba...

Debi: I FINALLY made my 'Ali-Booba'! As I was following the instructions I decided it would be really neat if I could actually make it feel like a real breast. As I was perusing the Dollar Store I came across Punch Balls, which are *similar to a balloon, but much thicker. I squeezed hair gel in to a punch ball, tied a knot, then inserted it in to a sock. I made the nipple the same way as the instructions you sent me. It feels just like a breast!! I also made a second one that I filled extra full so I could show moms what engorgement was like! I've already used them at work and the patients at first were quite amused, but then very receptive to them as a useful teaching tool.*

Socks can also be made into breastfeeding dolls; see Chapter 11.

The Happy Knappy or Dumpy Diaper

It's possible to knit efficient, eco-friendly nappies with wool containing lanolin, the sheep's natural waterproofing. But smaller ones can be used to explain the importance of their contents in the first few days, in conjunction with the NCT leaflet 'What's in a nappy?'[54] See Chapter 5 for a song to go with it.[*]

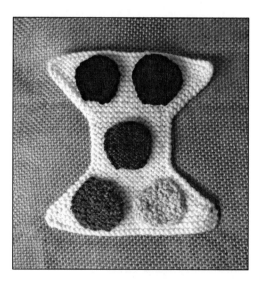

---

[*] Instructions for the sock breast and knappy are on my website: www.linkable.biz

18. A HANDY TOOLCHEST

Brief instructions:
Knit a modern-shaped nappy in garter stitch, and attach five coloured knitted or crocheted circles (about two inches in diameter) to represent the results of the first five days of feeding. They can be used to illustrate the song in Chapter 5.

Materials needed:
- white or cream yarn in chunky or double knitting
- size 7 or 8 needles
- small amounts of double or four-ply in various colours and textures
- size 10 needles or equivalent crochet hook

Stocking stitch gives a smooth effect, the reverse more textured. Moss stitch with a plain and bobbly wool mix works well for days four and five.

In antenatal classes, various foods on saucers can also be used to show changing colours and textures.

Day 1: black, smooth (Marmite)

Day 2: very dark green or black-green mix, smooth (dark avocado skin, plain cooked spinach)

Day 3: greeny-brown, somewhat more textured (curried spinach)

Day 4: browny-yellow with bobbles (grainy French mustard, wholenut peanut butter)

Day 5: golden yellow with bobbles (grainy English mustard, dry scrambled egg if bottlefed, as the poo is lighter in colour)

I explain to parents that if the poo is turning yellow by day three, all is going really well. But if it's still very dark, measures should be taken to increase the baby's input. I believe that using this sort of tool would vastly reduce the number of babies readmitted to neonatal units with excessive weight loss.

Knitwits

A global knitting revolution appears to be under way, judging by the number of websites giving weird and wonderful patterns for calculators, vacuum cleaners and toilet rolls. One knitter, known as Amybelbags, was troubled by noisy doors at home, so she made a 'Door Thing' to loop over the handles on either side. Her husband renamed these gadgets 'Door Thongs' – you can see why.[55]

A whole knitted digestive system appeared on the now-extinct website strangebuttrewe.com. The designer was Matie Trewe, who claimed to live in a tiny apartment in Eugene, Oregon with one loving fiancé and enough yarn to knit two more.

Chapter 19

The best medicine

Light relief

Packed lunch

Although I take my support of breastfeeding very seriously, I like to have a good laugh at the same time. Here are some updated medical definitions...

White's medical dictionary (companion to Black's)[56]

Artery – the study of paintings
Benign – what you be after you be eight
Bacteria – back entrance to café
Barium – what doctors do when patients die
Cauterize – chat-up preliminary
Dilate – live to a ripe old age
Nitrates – cheaper than day rates
Outpatient – one who has fainted

... which inspired me to write my own.

Blenk's maniacal lactionary

Inner desires regarding those who sabotage breastfeeding:
Strangyloglossia (especially those opposed to tongue-tie division)
Tongue tie (to stop further incorrect information)
Hand expression (non-verbal response)
Rejection reflex – attackment (skin to skin)
Nursing strike, with three-hourly thumping
Saw nipples

Possible feelings:
Let down

Resources:
Boxytocin (increases pains)
Scratch mitts for the (very) cross-cradle hold
Sling (as in David and Goliath)
Barrier method – to keep out detractors

19. THE BEST MEDICINE

Results:

Lactose (after stamping on feet)

Blocked ducts (respiratory)

Lying down position

Other definitions:

Ultrasound – good antenatal information on infant feeding

Global warming – skin-to-skin contact between breasts

Postpart 'em depression – difficulty in feeding caused by removal of baby at birth

Colostraphobia – fear of early feeding*

Colosstrum – lack of feeding in the first three days

Hitting the bottle – removing any need for supplements

C**p advice – false reassurance on lack of poo in the first week

Wait gain – delaying introduction of supplements while increasing effective breastfeeding

Phototherapy – the use of images to show good feeding positions

Thrive line – nursing supplementation system

Colic drops – high-fat milk from a well-drained breast

Suckcess – establishment of direct feeding

Hind milk – result of burping baby on the shoulder

Antibody – provided by a parent's sister for skin contact

Chest freezer – cooling breast pads

Between a rock and a hard place – baby's position when breasts are engorged

Open University degree – qualification needed to uncap painkillers

Tit for tat – use of breasts to promote sales of top-shelf magazines

Baby alarm – failing to use a human safety system

Purée – a food lower in calories than pure B (breastmilk)

---

* See Chapter 12

> *Spoon-feed – give advice that discourages parents from using common sense*
> *Dummy – someone who deters breastfeeders*
> *Blind – attitude of childcare guru* who recommends one for the nursery to teach good sleep habits*

Breasts on the keyboard

This is for anyone who spends hours on the computer. Most of the following were sent by LC Maud Giles in 2002, from a breast cancer awareness campaign in Australia. As lower breast cancer rates are associated with longer breastfeeding, it's appropriate to include them here.

> *Perfect breasts (o)(o)*
> *Fake silicone breasts (+)(+)*
> *Perky breasts (*)(*)*
> *Big nipple breasts (@)(@)*
> *A cups o o*
> *D cups { O }{ O }*
> *Wonderbra breasts (oYo)*
> *Cold breasts (^)(^)*
> *Lopsided breasts (o)(O)*
> *Pierced nipple breasts (O)(Q)*
> *Hanging tassels breasts (p)(p)*
> *Against the shower door breasts ( )( )*
> *Android breasts | o | | o |*
> *Mammogrammed breasts ____ ____*

I've added these:

> *Private boob job breasts (£)(£)*

---

*   Guru – Grossly Undermining Recommended Unity

Sore-nippled breasts with gauze dressings (#)(#)
Arabic film star breasts ح ح
Banned in public breasts Ø Ø
Breasts for twins 0< >0
Lopsided breasts % or ♫

Putting the fun into fundraising

Angel Tolentino in the USA uses her breasts to raise funds for breast cancer charities, as she explains on her website.

> *In December 1995, I was looking for creative Christmas gifts for my friends. One day I was watching my sister Lyn use sponges to paint on canvas. I thought, "I wonder if my breasts could work like sponges?" Inspiration struck! So I bought some non-toxic paint and canvas, locked myself in the bathroom, and figured out a technique to paint with my breasts. Wouldn't you know it? Breast Pals was born!*

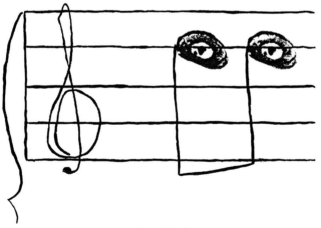

Double Ds

Listen and watch with mother in mind

Great Expectations
Doctor Dolittle
The Lady Vanishes
A Hard Day's Night
Latch of the Day
Left Side Story
Midnight Express
Sleepless on the Settee
The House at Pooh Corner
Monte Carlo or Bust
Twin Peaks
Golden Globe Awards

Find online

Why mums can't do yoga – a home video showing a baby whose world is turned upside down.

Chapter 20
The animal queendom

All about other mammals

Image courtesy of Lee Fearnley and Card Connection.

I started writing parodies of songs for our production of *Peter Pan-tomime* at senior school. Nearly thirty years and several hundred songs later, I composed a set for a church production of *Jack and the Beanstalk*. The cow was very upset by this threat.

> **Beef encounter**
> (tune: 'Daisy Bell' – or 'A bicycle made for two')
>
> *Daisy, Daisy,*
> *milk's needed, but there's none;*
> *you're just lazy,*
> *your lactating days are done.*
> *Your output of milk's so fickle*
> *we only get a trickle;*
> *if more's not squirted*
> *you'll be inserted*
> *into a McDonald's bun!*

Tigers, pigs, dogs, camels and elephants

A story on the internet tells of a tiger in a California zoo, who went into a decline after her three premature cubs died. She was given a litter of weaner pigs to restore her mood, and ended up nursing them. Images can be found on several websites by a search for 'tiger and piglets'. Although the photos are genuine, the story isn't. The zoo is in Thailand, and the reason for putting the animals together was to learn whether they would get on with each other.

The BBC News (Europe) site reported in November 2010 that a Spanish family's dog was nursing a piglet after it was rejected by the butcher for being too small for Christmas dinner.[57]

The film *The Weeping Camel* is a beautiful documentary about life in the Gobi desert. A newborn camel is rejected after a long and difficult birth. The family call in a violinist to soothe the mother. Haunting music and songs enable her to accept the colt, and as her milk begins to flow, so do her tears.

Another film, *Echo – An Unforgettable Elephant,* follows the long life of an African elephant. When one of her calves, Ely, was born, he couldn't straighten his legs. Echo and her daughter Enid stood over him for three days, until at last he could stand up to nurse. At the time of writing, clips of this caring behaviour could be seen on the BBC website under the title 'Echo the African bush elephant'. The film showed another of her babies sucking his own trunk, then folding it back to take his mother's teats, placed (like ours) on the chest rather than abdomen.

Open for lunch

On a visit to a small zoo in south-west England, I watched a lemur nursing her baby. As I stepped forward to take a photograph, she raised her long stripy tail and covered her front, just as a human mother might use a shawl for privacy. The sow I met on a farm later wasn't at all bothered to hide herself away.

Going bananas
For many years, baby doll sets such as 'Tiny Tears'
have included bottles and dummies. Now one toy
manufacturer has gone a stage further. The 'FurReal Friends
Cuddle Chimp' comes with a banana-shaped feeding bottle.

The true behaviour of nursing mammals makes for fascinating study. The following extract is used with permission from the book *Breastfeeding at a Glance*. [58]

How Do Other Mammals Nurse?

Days and nights we stayed up in the bracken pile,
curled around one another, while I gave suck and
licked and settled squabbles. They fed and slept and
fed and squabbled, and I watched their small, sleek
bodies plumping up with milk. Their eyes were shut,
their small heads pushed into my flank, muzzles
butting, jaws working hard in the rhythm of life,
which is, at first, no more than suck and swallow.

From *Fire, Bed & Bone*, Henrietta Branford,
Candlewick Press, 1998

There are over 4,200 species of mammals on our planet. Mammals are animals that have a backbone, have hair or fur, are warm-blooded and whose females nurse their babies with milk. Each of these milks contains water, proteins, fats, carbohydrates, minerals, vitamins, cellular content and anti-infective agents. But each species of mammal produces a milk that is qualitatively different than the milk of other species, a milk that is perfectly suited for the growth and development of the offspring of that particular species.

The composition of the milk is related to the rate of growth of a species. Human milk is low in both protein and fat. Mammals with high fat content generally have young who need to form a thick coat of blubber to protect them from the cold. Mammals with a high protein content generally have young where growth is rapid and the young mature in a short time. Humans are among the slowest growing of all mammals.

Percent Protein and Fat in Milk

Species	% Protein	% Fat
Human	0.9	3.8
Talapoin monkey	2.1	3.0
Goat	2.9	4.5
Cow	3.4	3.7
African elephant	4.0	5.0
Black bear	7.0	25.1
Little brown bat	8.5	15.8
Gray seal	9.2	59.8
Cat	10.6	10.8
Blue whale	11.9	40.9
House mouse	12.5	27.0

One important feature of all non-human mammals is that they suckle their young until they are able to become independent. Breastfeeding is the crucial bridge between infancy and maturity. Here's how some different mammals breastfeed...

Mammal Lactation Trivia

1. The female duck-billed platypus breastfeeds without benefit of a breast or a nipple. The mammary glands rest underneath the mother's chest. The youngster pushes

against the chest wall with his soft, pliable bill, then licks the oozing milk off his mother's skin and hair.

2. Whales need to preserve their sleek, hydrodynamically efficient shape. The mother's milk glands are below her thick blubber layer. This inside location also protects the milk from cold. The baby nudges the area and milk – thick as cream – spurts out. A baby Pacific gray whale can drink 80 pounds of breastmilk a day.

3. Hippos are born underwater – and nurse underwater, too. The mother puts her head under water and boosts the newborn to the surface to breathe. Then the baby goes under again, finds a nipple and suckles, instinctively folding down his ears and closing his nostrils. Every twenty to forty seconds, he bobs to the surface to breathe and swallow.

4. Female and young lions live together in a pride. In one pride, all the lionesses take care of all the cubs. Unlike almost all other mammals, any lioness will wet-nurse any cub. A napping lioness who has been hunting all night doesn't pay much attention to who is suckling on her. And because they are all so closely related, a lioness helps the family no matter whose baby she nurses.

5. The hooded seal lives about thirty years, but spends only four days nursing and being a child, the shortest nursing period of any mammal. They live at sea, but they must give birth and nurse out of the water. The only surface available is floating ice. Pups are born when the ice is beginning to melt and break up. A sudden storm

might send pieces crashing together, crushing moms and pups. Or an ice floe might split, and moms and pups could be separated. A short childhood helps avoid these perils.

6. Orangutans breastfeed, ride on their mother's body and sleep in her nest for seven years – among the longest nursing period of any mammal. The young stay with their mothers at least until a new baby arrives; males begin to wander off then, but females may stay around for a while observing how babies are cared for. They are accomplished acrobats, often nursing upside down – hanging by a hand and a foot from a branch.

7. Baby animals are weaned when the mother is newly pregnant or preparing for another pregnancy. In western culture, today, the most common reason cited for human weaning is in preparation to return to a job outside the home.[58]

You'll have to stop – the Nanny Agency wants me back

Chapter 21

Making savings

How breastfeeding saves lives and commerce damages them

Imagine if today, scientists discovered a drug that could save 13 percent of all the babies who currently die. Now imagine that drug also made your baby cleverer – and dramatically slashed her chances of developing heart disease, diabetes, leukaemia, asthma or obesity as an adult. The "drug" exists. It is called breast milk.[59]

At the end of 2008 the journal of the Royal College of Midwives published an article about the challenges of meeting the fifth of the United Nations' eight Millennium Development Goals (MDGs). MDG5 is concerned with reducing maternal mortality. Although it stresses the need for effective contraception, it makes no mention of the effect of lactation on fertility. In response, I wrote an article entitled 'Breastfeeding saves mothers' lives', pointing out that the promotion and protection of breastfeeding directly addresses seven of the MDGs, including the issue of contraception. The article was published in *Midwives* in April 2009 and can be read online.[60]

Protecting the breast

One result of a lack of breastfeeding is an increase in breast cancer risk, both for the mothers, and also for their daughters in later life.

This risk is linked with the number of menstrual periods in a woman's lifetime. I was intrigued by a discussion of this issue in one of Malcolm Gladwell's essays in the book *What the Dog Saw*. 'John Rock's Error' refers to a study of the Dogon tribe in Mali in the 1980s. This revealed that childbearing begins soon after puberty at around sixteen years; babies are breastfed well into their second year or beyond; and contraceptive devices are not used. Dogon women typically have about 100 periods during their lives, whereas Western women are used to having three to four times that number. Such frequency is clearly biologically abnormal, and this raises questions about the safety of birth control pills that maintain monthly bleeding.[61]

It's sobering to realise how much our dietary habits and child-bearing practices contribute to the nation's incidence of breast cancer (and incidentally boost the profits of the sanitary protection industry). Cancer Research UK states that breastfeeding every child for an extra six months would mean about 1,000 fewer cases of breast cancer in Britain each year. Unfortunately, a lot of information about breast cancer, such as an article on the UK website www.netdoctor.co.uk, fails to mention lactation as one factor in keeping the risk of this disease low.[62]

One Million Campaign

As more becomes known about this and many other risks of a lack of breastfeeding, calls for its protection have been increasing. In May 2009, IBFAN, the International Baby Food Action Network, launched its 'One Million Campaign: Support Women to Breastfeed' at the World Health Assembly. By the autumn of 2010 it had amassed more than 141,300 petitioners.[63]

Another organisation, Deliver Now for Women and Children, was set up by WHO in 2007 to address the shocking fact that a woman dies in childbirth every minute, and a child under four dies every three seconds. Of these children, four million die in their first month, three in four of these during the first week.

21. MAKING SAVINGS

Mythbusting

Research shows that if babies breastfeed in the first hour of life, their chance of survival is greatly increased compared with those put to the breast later. But in many countries like Pakistan and India, the early milk is thought to be dangerous. Deliver Now created a film showing young Indian mothers watching a TV programme. The TV doctor advises them to give 'colostrum' rather than honey water to keep their babies healthy. The women search the market stalls in vain for this wonderful product. Eventually they approach a holy man who says, 'Look inside yourselves; you will surely find it.' The mothers then come face to face with the TV doctor and find out that colostrum is *kasha kheera*, which they have always believed to be harmful. The doctor explains that every drop has more power than any other food, and that breastfeeding exclusively for six months will keep their babies healthy. This witty and sensitive approach has proved effective in changing attitudes and practices.[64]

Such campaigns, like the Nestlé boycott mentioned below, are necessary because of the power of the babyfood industry.

There's no milk like mum's milk

When animals can't get their mother's milk, great care is needed to find a suitable alternative. My nephew Pete's wife Lorisa is an expert in this field. She works at the York Centre for Wildlife in Maine, USA, and uses the basement at home as a rehabilitation space. In the image overleaf she is syringe-feeding an abandoned woodchuck.

Replacement feeding for human youngsters has not received the same care; if it had, cows might never have been used as mother-substitute. Bovine milk is known to be less suited to humans than that of sheep, goats and donkeys. Indeed, Italy is already promoting the donkey variety as a healthier option, despite its high cost. But current European legislation does not permit standard infant formula to be based on supplies from animals other than the cow. This is because they are most easily engineered to deliver vast quantities, so their milk has practically monopolised the market.

Although there is no evidence that any mammal needs milk beyond childhood, adult humans in the West consume so much dairy produce that indoor 'mega-dairies' for hundreds of cows have been proposed to cope with the demand. The organisation Compassion in World Farming gives more details on its website about the effect this will have on the unfortunate occupants.

Cow's milk allergy is very common. Many people are concerned about the link between dairy products and other health problems, such as cancer and diabetes. Soya 'milk' is thought by many to carry unwarranted risks to health too. But the babymilk industry, which is based on these products, is booming. Why?

21. MAKING SAVINGS

Matters of interest

It is only recently that concerns over artificial feeding have been drowned out by commercial interests. Until the twentieth century, there was a general consensus that breastmilk substitutes were dangerous. At the 22nd World Congress of Paediatrics in 1980, Professor Peter Dunn gave a slide talk on the importance of breast-feeding and human milk. He included this statement:

> Many years ago Ambrose Bierce (nineteenth-century journalist and author of The Devil's Dictionary) defined mammalia as a family of vertebrate animals whose females suckle their young in a state of nature, but when civilised and enlightened put them out to nurse or use the bottle.[65]

FORMULA: Feed Of Replacement Milk Using Legalised Alternatives

Until the middle of the last century, it was common for babies to be fed 'doorstep' milk, with or without crude modification, or recon-stituted evaporated milk. The development of more appropriate breastmilk substitutes came about partly as a result of pressure from groups like Baby Milk Action, which gives guidance in using formula on its website.[66] But the popularity of these highly modified 'infant' milks has been created and driven by commerce rather than health concerns. Company promotion, both aggressive and subtle, has resulted in the bottle becoming one of the most widely recognised symbols of babyhood in the UK.*

Nutritionist Gabrielle Palmer's brilliant and disturbing book *The Politics of Breastfeeding* leaves us in no doubt about why natural feeding has been sabotaged over the last hundred years. Its main root is an unholy alliance made between the medical profession and

---

* See the cartoon in Chapter 9.

artificial milk manufacturers at the end of the nineteenth century. This marriage (similar to that enacted between doctors and pharmaceutical companies) is still alive and well, raking in profits for a few and misery for many.

So it's not surprising that many hospital staff act as though artificial babymilk is the answer to every feeding problem. I wrote my first lactation song in 1998 to express my frustration at this situation. A year later, I used it to lighten the mood among my fellow candidates just before we took the LC exam. Fortunately, the practice of passing a stomach tube to wash out mucus and give formula seems less prevalent now.

I omit the names of the milks here, but include them when I sing it!

Hitting the bottle
(tune: 'Don't bring Lulu')

Bad advice

If baby's weight is low or great then give a bottle;
if you need a rest, don't give your breast, just give a bottle.
If your baby likes to cry
and your breasts feel high and dry,
you don't need to feed all day –
open up the * * A.
(You should never hesitate –
give a drink of * * Gate.)

If baby's yellow, hear us bellow
"Give a bottle!"
If feeds are few 'cos there's some mucus,
tube-feed 30 mls;
if baby is too sleepy,
there's no need to get weepy,

give a bottle, this is what'll
cure all baby's ills!

Baby Friendly version

If you want to breastfeed well then give just breastmilk;
if your baby likes to yell then give more breastmilk.
Every time your baby feeds
you will make the milk he needs;
if today lactation's poor
by tomorrow there'll be more.

Every cue for hunger heed,
and give just breastmilk;
if at first you don't succeed
you will at last excel.
Today you may be tearful,
but soon you'll both be cheerful –
give just breastmilk,
it's the best milk
to keep your baby well!

Guilt complex

We are often told that women should not feel guilty if they have to use formula milk. However, research shows that bottle-feeding is not a personal choice for many mothers today, but the only option when breastfeeding is not supported. They often feel guilt rather than a more appropriate anger. My aim has never been to make women breastfeed, or to feel bad if they don't, but to make it possible for them to have a real choice. The vast majority of bottle-feeding mothers I have met wanted to nurse their babies, but the difficulties they encountered, or fears raised by others' experiences, seemed insurmountable. A Western view of the role of the breast exacerbates these problems.

This song was written by BFC Charlotte Thomas.

What are they for?
(tune: 'Heads, shoulders knees and toes' – repeat
ends of first, second and fourth lines as in original)

Breasts in papers line the shops,
breasts on billboards, skimpy tops,
and breasts on beaches out on show;
What are breasts for? do you know?

I think that some perhaps forgot
(the formula companies helped a lot)
that monkeys, cats and even camels
are all like us, and we're Mammals.

'Mammal' means that milk we make
is on tap for babe to take.
So why then now in modern age
is bottle-feeding all the rage?

Did women's breasts break over time?
Did breastmilk then get less sublime?
Did something better come along?
Maybe nature got it wrong!

Alas, the answer's sadly not,
nothing's changed, no not a jot,
at least in terms of women's breasts
and doing what they do the best.

The other is poor substitute
(which evidence does not refute),

increasing risk of death and disease,
cancers, SIDS, and being obese.

For this the parents have to pay
a pound or two, but every day!
It then needs making, every feed,
at 3am, not what you need!

With babies dying every day
I really think it's time to say,
"Give women the support they need
to feed their babies AND succeed!"

Gift rap

Babyfood companies get health professionals to advertise their products by providing 'free' items such as stationery, calendars and obstetric date wheels. A consultant paediatrician told me in all seriousness that he supported one company because it gave him free pens. Poor man! The industry subsidises study days, and uses dedicated websites to draw in practitioners. In the summer of 2010, one company offered midwives educational funding of £25,000 through Tommy's, a charitable organisation devoted to pregnancy health.[67] (One might reasonably question whether its concern for babies' health extends beyond birth.) Commenting on the story in the Baby Milk Action campaign blog, Mike Brady considers that this company is using Tommy's to handle the money in an attempt to make it more acceptable.[68]

Current UK legislation requires all babymilk packaging to include a message that breastfeeding is best for babies. This gives the impression that the companies support it; but if they don't get babies on the bottle, they don't do business. The law is powerless to prevent many other messages that successfully undermine natural feeding. Some years ago, a well-known manufacturer distributed postcards showing a mother holding a baby, with the caption "I'm thinking of getting a t-shirt made – Danger! Sore boobs!" The card encouraged mothers to call the careline or visit the website if they had breast-feeding difficulties.[69]

The wonderful cartoonist Richard Willson clarifies the role of the babymilk producer.

The origin of the Milky Way, after Tintoretto

This is my response to these companies.

There's nothing like the breast!
(tune: 'I've got a little list' from *The Mikado*
– but better recited)

*The babymilk producers claim that cow's milk bottle-feeds
give total nourishment for infant aliment;*

that vitamins and minerals are what a baby needs,
with fat at four per cent to keep him quite content.
They've added beta-carotene, infection to subdue,
and long-chain polyunsaturated fatty acids too;
if baby's sleep and feeding patterns ever get deranged,
the whey and casein ratio can easily be changed,
and if there's dairy allergy, then soya milk is good,
providing tasty food for healthy babyhood.
The companies attest that mother's milk is best,
but their own has passed the test as substitute for breast.

But let's examine carefully what human milk provides
when little ones request a drink from Mummy's breast;
because it's rich in lysozyme and oligo-saccharides,
immunity's possessed, and pathogens suppressed.
With leucocytes and macrophages, very much alive,
and iron-binding lactoferrin, bugs will never thrive.
The milk at every nursing is more watery at first,
so small and frequent feeds in summer quench a baby's thirst;
endorphins then ensure that both will have a peaceful rest,
so babes are very blessed by mother's treasure chest.
The milk producers' quest to mimic nature's best
therefore fails to pass the test – there's nothing like the breast!

The Code

All formula manufacturers currently contravene the International Code of Marketing of Breastmilk Substitutes (the Code), adopted by the World Health Assembly in 1981. Their promotions contribute to the yearly toll of around 1.5 million baby deaths caused by a lack of breastfeeding. Visit Baby Milk Action's website for more details. Developing countries, of course, are hardest hit.

Pakistan's situation

In the hospital in Bannu where I was based for thirteen years, I frequently saw the dire consequences of too little breastfeeding. Although nearly all mothers nursed their newborns, they were bombarded by formula adverts on TV and billboards, and in hospitals and doctors' surgeries. Pictures of plump, fair-skinned babies on the tins gave a strong impression that the product was healthy and beneficial. Under most conditions, it was anything but that.

Many mothers could not read; education for girls was almost unheard of in the tribal areas nearby. They didn't know that boiled water and sterile equipment was needed, and anyway, fuel for cooking was very expensive, as was the milk powder. Feeds reconstituted with dirty water to an eighth of the recommended strength, and given by filthy bottles and teats, often caused severe gastroenteritis and led to terrible malnutrition. To treat diarrhoea, some health workers told parents to dilute the milk further, and then give only water, and then nothing at all. Eventually the diarrhoea did stop – and also the baby's breathing. However, another baby would probably already be on the way, because cessation of frequent breastfeeding had resulted in a return to fertility.* Such frequent pregnancies put the mother's own health at risk.

This sad situation persists in many parts of Pakistan. Although the country is a signatory to the Code, a report by the Associated Press of Pakistan in July 2010 showed that babymilk companies were still breaking the rules. However, matters are improving. Many local doctors now recognise the huge risks of artificial feeding, and a large proportion of hospitals have been designated Baby Friendly. TheNetwork, a Pakistani consumer organisation, has been working to promote normal feeding since 1996. Its website proclaims: 'Protection of Breastfeeding is single most effective measure in combating infant mortality in Pakistan'. As a result of TheNetwork's

* See Chapter 12

advocacy and hard work, the Ministry of Health enacted legislation to outlaw formula promotion in February 2010.When I contacted its Project Co-ordinator Rubina Bhatti to congratulate the group, she told me that public advertising had lessened as a result. However, she was deeply concerned about the influence of companies on health workers, which meant that many children were still being bottle-fed on a doctor's recommendation.

Milking public sympathy

You can imagine how such advice would affect young lives in the terrible monsoon floods of 2010, which occurred while I was preparing the second edition of this book.A report in *The Guardian* newspaper in early September, entitled 'Behind the photograph: the human face of Pakistan's deadly flood', showed a homeless, malnourished two-year-old sucking an empty bottle. His mother – who had eight children under the age of nine – said it had been weeks since Reza and his twin brother had tasted milk. Two days later, the paper reported that a worldwide response to this story had enabled delivery of foodstuffs, including milk. A photo showed Reza drinking some of it from a bottle.

The article did not mention the Emergency Nutrition Network's 'Guidelines for Infant and Young Child Feeding in Emergencies', which spells out the risks of bottle-feeding in such a situation. An online discussion under this story included concerns about formula donations in emergencies, provoking a complaint that the story had been 'hijacked by the breastfeeding mafia'.* Fortunately, Ali Maclaine, a breastfeeding advocate with an MSc in Human Nutrition, stepped into the discussion with more information about these guidelines. Two weeks after the story was run, the paper published a response from Unicef underlining the dangers of promoting bottle-feeding, but the damage had already been done.

---

* See Chapter 22 for a song about this inappropriate term.

Fighting the Nestlé monster

Nestlé, the largest babyfood company and worst flouter of the Code, has been the subject of a global boycott for many years. Tony and I spotted this bin at a campsite in Kent. It shows what many of us think of Nestlé, and our only possible response to its products – REFUSE!

Baby Milk Action's website gives more details about Nestlé's activities and the many reasons for concern. This song is dedicated to all those who support the boycott, and calls for others to join in.

Boycott Nestlé!
(tune: 'Men of Harlech')

Nestlé makes confectionery,
chocolates plain and white and dairy;
should you eat them, or be wary?
You must now decide.
Mums who've chosen natural feeding
may find Nestlé's ads misleading,
and assume that they'll be needing
bottled milk beside.

Milk of cow's creation,
and factory adaptation,
needing boiled and measured water,

sterile bottles and refrigeration.
If these cannot be afforded,
of their babies' health they'll be defrauded;
they may find their trust rewarded
with infanticide.

There is evidence compelling
Nestlé's constantly rebelling
against the global Code of selling
by such companies.
Nestlé's really quite inventive,
giving staff a cash incentive
to ensure they stay attentive
to its policies.

And it keeps devising
subtle advertising
to promote its babymilk
to nurses and the mothers they're advising;
acting on false information
may result in failure of lactation.
Help us stop this violation –
boycott Nestlé, please!

Law and disorder

The Code was adopted by the World Health Assembly in 1981 as a minimum requirement to protect infant health. All babyfood companies should abide by the Code, even if their country of operation has not adopted it as legislation. Britain has far weaker regulations, and even these are systematically flouted. Promotion of first stage milk (including price reductions) is banned, but stores may use eye-catching messages about baby products right above the shelves of formula, perhaps to get round this ban. Adverts often sneak into parenting magazines and online grocery sites. In 2009, a promotion for one brand of first stage milk appeared in millions of Tesco Direct catalogues. I was one of many who protested to Trading Standards; no prosecutions were brought against either the store or the company.

Companies outdo each other in making health claims (allowed under UK law) about their milks. Their adverts appear in many medical, nursing and midwifery publications (also allowed), implying general professional endorsement. This idealisation of formula use as beneficial, without mentioning the risks to health, greatly increases those risks. Even children are targeted by the industry. I know of a school which was given branded sports equipment by a large pharmaceutical company. A representative explained to the children that the company produced things to make people better, and gave, as an example, the name of its babymilk.

In the summer of 2010, the National Childbirth Trust reported that a GCSE science exam question (set for fourteen- to sixteen-year-old schoolchildren) promoted donations of formula in emergencies, pouring scorn on international marketing standards and the charitable sector that seeks to uphold them. The NCT, deeply concerned that the babymilk industry might be implicated in such bias, called for a detailed investigation into commercial influence on exam papers.

Here's a closer look at these so-called healthy products.

Airy-fairy dairy – scary!
(tune: 'Who will buy?' from *Oliver!*)

Who will buy this formula powder?
it's designed to liberate mums;
simply shake it up in a bottle
and pour it into hungry tums.
But let's explore this product's history –
its founder was a cow;
to mimic human milk's a mystery,
but let's imagine how.

First remove two-thirds of the sodium,
then the fat, it's bad for the heart;
mix with oil from fish-eyes or seaweed,
and modify the protein part.
Increase the sweetness with corn syrup,
add iron and vitamins,
ensure that pre- and pro-biotics
are labelled on the tins.

What a lot of fancy ingredients!
Let's see what it cannot supply –
antigens and mother's own flavours;
but even though it's true
that benefits are few,
the ads bring many who will buy!

While I am infuriated by these commercial tactics, I am not against using artificial babymilk when it is needed. In our present situation, it is essential for some babies' wellbeing. But it is scandalous that replacements of the only food specifically designed for infants are treated so casually.

Market research

The Baby Feeding Law Group (BFLG), administered by Baby Milk Action, monitors the babyfood industry and works to bring UK marketing regulations into line with international standards. This would protect all babies. BFLG continues to call on the government to simplify the UK regulations, and save money, by adopting the Code and curbing the promotion of babymilk.

Breastmilk squeezes out formula sales

The Food Commission, an independent watchdog, reported with heavy irony in The Food Magazine in 2006:

Selfish breastfeeding mums are costing baby food companies a fortune in profits every year. If every one of the approximately 720,000 babies born in the UK each year were formula fed, that would mean around £350 million in sales for companies selling milk powder, sterilisers, bottles and all of the many other bits and pieces that go along with bottle-feeding. And companies are so good at it, what mum could begrudge them the £500 it costs to feed her baby a year?[70]

Let's look on the bright side. The Breastfeeding Manifesto, launched by Best Beginnings' founder Alison Baum in 2006, was produced in consultation with over twenty UK organisations working to reduce health inequalities. It is now supported by a coalition of more than thirty professional and lay groups. Individuals and organisations can show their support by signing up to the Manifesto's seven objectives, one of which is to adopt the Code as UK legislation.

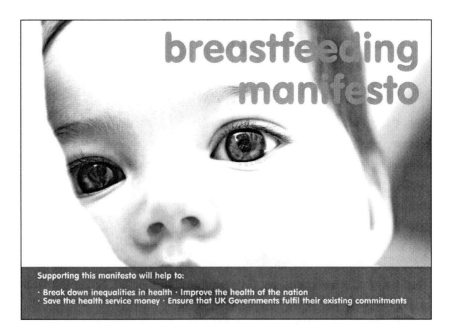

breastfeeding
manifesto

Supporting this manifesto will help to:

· Break down inequalities in health · Improve the health of the nation
· Save the health service money · Ensure that UK Governments fulfil their existing commitments

Chapter 22

Get it off your chest

The scandal of misinformation

Good communication is vital, as misunderstandings can easily arise.

I'M QUITE HAPPY WITH THE ONE
I'VE GOT, ACTUALLY

The formula industry has a lot of help from other agencies in undermining facts about infant feeding. Some completely reverse the sense of a message. I have a front cover of a newspaper magazine showing a lovely picture of a baby at the breast, to illustrate an article written in 2005 entitled 'Know when to stop, or just go with the flow?' The article was written by two parenting specialists disputing the appropriate term of breastfeeding, while acknowledging its intrinsic value. However, the huge caption under the cover photo reads 'WHY BREAST IS NOT BEST'.

Watering down the facts

In 2004, the pharmacy chain Boots began selling flavoured water for babies from four weeks of age. When I complained to the company that this was both unnecessary and potentially harmful, I was told that babies found flavoured water 'more palatable' than plain boiled water. The label was later altered to show it as suitable from four months, although even bottle-fed babies don't usually need water for at least six months.

In 2005 some information from the Department of Health trickled out about the need for powdered formula to be made up with hot water. The instructions were very unclear, such as the advice to 'boil a kettle and leave it to cool for half an hour'. I wrote to the Food Standards Agency for clarification on the safe temperature range, and received the following reply many weeks later:

> We asked Department of Health about this, but I'm afraid
> they don't have any information on this topic. Sorry not
> to be able to give you the answer you're looking for – all
> I can suggest is that you try contacting some formula
> manufacturers.

Many childcare publications, written by both professional and unqualified authors, should be catalogued as Comic Fiction. The British Medical Association 'Family Doctor' series of booklets included one entitled 'Understanding: Infant Feeding'. This stated that both formula and breastmilk are unsuitable for babies over one year old. Fortunately, that title is now unavailable. But the NHS has continued the trend for misinformation, for example stating that there are advantages to bottle-feeding over breastfeeding, and that breastfeeding is contra-indicated with maternal Hepatitis B infection. I have been trying for years to correct such errors on Government sites covering infant feeding. At the time of writing, one page on NHS Choices showed my complaint about its content in the comments section![71]

Visit the Hathor the Cow Goddess website for many cartoons about similar frustrations.

> **The Daily Telegraph**'s medical column, apparently written by a real doctor, was once headlined 'It's not much fun being a baby these days'. Referring to the Department of Health's advice for babies to be exclusively breastfed for six months, he wrote, "Mother's milk is scarcely very appetising – it tastes like skimmed cow's milk fortified with several teaspoonfuls of sugar."

Embarrassing mistakes

Doctors and popular authors are readily believed by the general public, even when their pronouncements have no basis in fact. Dr Hilary Jones stated on a breakfast TV programme in February 2008: "After the age of one, breastfeeding is bizarre, unusual and not necessary. At four years it is not valid nutritionally." On a similar programme in January 2010, self-styled expert Clare Byam-Cook told the nation that human milk causes dental decay. In a discussion with Ann Sinnott, author of *Breastfeeding Older Children*, she said: "Breastmilk beyond the age of two isn't necessarily good because it's very, very sweet. The fact that it's breastmilk doesn't make it any better than a glass of Coca-Cola." This provoked a mixture of fury and derision among the many people who know that human milk does not rot baby teeth.

Dr Christian Jessen of the Channel 4 TV show *Embarrassing Bodies*, who stated that children need no milk of any kind after the age of one, also wrote an article for a women's magazine headed 'Breastfeeding can make your boobs sag – FACT!'* He also made similar comments to women featured on the show. Dr Jessen's 'expert' remarks, which were contradicted by one of his co-presenters on the C4 website, caused a storm of protest from those who know better. However, the Press Complaints Commission did not consider its code had been breached by the written publications.

Such comments can have a devastating effect. In the summer of 2010, a baby product review site, BabyChild.org.uk, polled over 1,000 young women for their attitudes to breastfeeding. The survey, which was reported by the Royal College of Midwives, showed that half of them planned to bottle-feed, largely for fear of

> *Nursing does not diminish the beauty of a woman's breasts; it enhances their charm by making them look lived in and happy.*
>
> Robert A. Heinlein

'ruining the look of their breasts'. Most believed that breastmilk substitutes would have no impact on their baby's health. Valerie Finigan's book *Saggy Boobs and Other Breastfeeding Myths* aims to counteract such lack of knowledge with gentle humour.

Mythinformation

The law appears inadequate to protect the vulnerable from such ignorant pronouncements. BFC Anne Simmance, creator of the Dispelling Breastfeeding Myths project, has set up a petition to the

---

* As sagging happens over time, watching enough rubbish on TV could also do it.

PCC for 'special guidelines concerning the coverage of breastfeeding issues in the press, to encourage balanced reporting of all the health issues related to breastfeeding and formula feeding.'[72]

Such guidelines are also needed for audio and visual media. In 2007, Channel 4 TV aired a documentary entitled *Bringing up Baby*. Over three programmes, parents were shown trying out different methods of childcare recommended by Dr Truby King in the 1950s, Dr Benjamin Spock in the 1960s, and author Jean Liedloff in the 1970s. One of the 'experts' advising the parents was a woman named Claire Verity, who described herself as a maternity nurse with accredited training and much experience. She was filmed ordering mothers to leave their newborns alone for hours, feed them to a strict schedule, and limit cuddling to ten minutes a day. This provoked outrage among professional and lay viewers alike.

A subsequent investigation showed that Ms Verity had no childcare qualifications; she was completely discredited, leaving the TV company with egg on its face. I would like to think that the parents featured in the programme, and others who were encouraged to follow this advice, were offered compensation by Channel 4, but I have no reason to believe that this happened.

Stories to make your hair curl

Many women worry about their ability to breastfeed. This isn't surprising, as many myths have been perpetuated throughout the last century. One of them, which I have heard many times, is that women with red hair and pale skin are more likely to get sore nipples. Some are even told that they can't breastfeed. I heard of one such mother in Germany, who reluctantly put her daughter on the bottle. When she moved to Canada, she found support to breastfeed her next two children. But another Canadian mother, as LC Sarah Brown reported in Treasure Chest in 2003, was also told she'd better forget breastfeeding, as she had red hair. When she pointed out that it was dyed, the answer was still the same!

Message in a bottle

Newspapers and other media often use images of bottle-feeding to illustrate any old story about babies. The Conservative Party, complaining about high levels of debt incurred by the ruling Labour Party, posted a video on YouTube in January 2009 showing a baby drinking from a bottle. Many complained, not least because of the unsafe way the baby was being fed, flat on his back with no adult in view. When the Tories returned to shared power in 2010, I wrote to my MP again to get the video clip removed, but to no avail. Later that year, newspapers put photos of the Prime Minister bottle-feeding his own baby on their front pages, and a BBC TV documentary showed the leader of the opposition in a supermarket, naively (and probably illegally) promoting the brand of formula he was giving his newborn.

In the autumn of 2010, the BBC news and website showed a photo of a baby drinking from a bottle in a story about changes in child benefit payments. When I complained about the damaging effect of such images on the public's view of infant feeding, I received this response by email:

> We use a range of pictures on stories, including ones
> where babies are fed this way. It is a commonly
> recognisable image of parenthood...

Going on the offensive

2007 was a good year for rants against breastfeeding supporters. 'Breast may not be best after all' was the title for a newspaper report on research showing an apparent link between breastfeeding and asthma. The article accused 'breastfeeding zealots' of turning BF promotion into a moral crusade. Supporters are still regularly described as the Nipple Police, the Breastfeeding Mafia, the Breastapo and even Nazis. These last two, especially, are deeply offensive in their trivialisation of the horror faced by victims of the Holocaust. And far from killing six million people, BF supporters are calling for life-saving measures. The next song honours their work.

Mafia?
(tune: 'Maria', from *West Side Story*)

Mafia – we've just been described as Mafia!
Could anything be worse
than helping mothers nurse their child?
Mafia – how can we be known as Mafia?
Did we commit a crime
in giving mothers time to smile?
Mafia! We're not bullies with strident voices,
but we long to enable true choices.
Mafia – we wish you'd stop saying Mafia!

Some mothers do experience undue pressure to breastfeed, but in my experience such coercion only comes from those whose keenness isn't matched by comprehensive BF education. No one with adequate training belittles a mother who has chosen or been obliged to use formula, or fails to understand why she might be in this situation.

Breastfeeding falsies

"Breast is best but formula is perfectly healthy"

"Breastfeeding always hurts at first"

"Your nipples need to toughen up"

"Premature babies always need fortified milk"

"She's a small baby, you'll need to give her a top-up"

"He's a big baby, you'll need to give him a top-up"

"Babies need to learn to take a bottle"

237

"If you have a low supply, you need to eat more"

"Breastmilk loses its goodness after xxx months"

Some women complain that they are made to feel guilty for not breastfeeding. In an online debate on breastfeeding and IQ one such mother signed herself thus:
Bottle Babe, Brest, France.

Chapter 23

Every home should have some

Other uses for real milk

In 2006, I wrote to *The Times* Body & Soul section's resident GP Keith Hopcroft, to add breastmilk to his 'Home Remedies'. I explained that it could be used to treat various conditions such as baby's sticky eyes and snuffly noses. My letter appeared under the title 'Mother's milk – a panacea'. The doctor agreed that it was useful for baby's exterior as well as interior needs, adding that it could also treat warts.

The following advice for treating all-age problems, including warts, comes from Liz Laing in Los Angeles.[73] (Note that untreated breastmilk should not be used outside one's own family.)

> **Cuts, Scrapes, Scratches** Clean wound first using breastmilk if you don't have soap and water. Drip milk onto the wound, then let it air-dry. You can also use a cotton ball or a 4-by-4-inch gauze pad soaked in breastmilk. If the cut is on a baby's lips or mouth area, allow him or her to nurse. An upset child will be calmed by the gentle, loving act of breastfeeding, and the milk will help heal the wound.
>
> **Diaper Rash** Gently pat baby's bottom with breastmilk, being especially generous when applying it to reddened or rash areas. Leave baby's diaper off for a few minutes and let the bottom air-dry.

Ear Infections Place a few drops of breastmilk in the ear; follow with warm (not hot) olive oil and garlic, or bottled garlic mullein oil (sold at natural food stores).

Red or Puffy Eyes Place two cotton balls saturated with breastmilk over closed eyes for a few minutes – works better than tea bags or cucumber slices!

Insect Bites With a clean finger, dab breastmilk on the bite; this will help stop the itching.

Skin Rash/Wounds Apply breastmilk on itchy spots – even chickenpox – for soothing relief. One woman claims that she used her breastmilk to clear up an elderly relative's leg ulcers. It's also possible that breastmilk helps heal skin wounds in nursing women themselves.

Sore or Cracked Nipples Gently rub milk onto nipples or area of soreness and let air-dry. Another option is to bathe the sore nipple by dipping it into a clean, shallow dish of breastmilk.

Sore Throats Baby can benefit by directly nursing.

Warts Leave a breastmilk-saturated cotton ball on the wart for a few minutes twice a day. Continue for several days until the wart dries up.

Other uses for breastmilk include dabbing it on perineal tears and stitches, acne spots, shaving cuts, minor burns, and indeed any place where a soothing lotion is needed.

23. EVERY HOME SHOULD HAVE SOME

There are more things in breastmilk, Horatio, than are dreamt of ...

Breastfeeding is known to keep the risk of childhood malignancies low. Some years ago, scientists suggested that human milk could also be used to treat cancer in adults. A substance called HAMLET - Human Alpha-lactalbumin Made Lethal to Tumour cells - was discovered by chance while Swedish researchers were investigating the antibacterial properties of breastmilk. An internet search brings up several stories of adults fighting cancer with donated breastmilk, despite scepticism by their doctors.

However, more research was published in 2010 to verify this treatment. HAMLET has been tested in humans, and is now known to kill forty types of cancer cell, leaving healthy cells undamaged.[74]

A fitting conclusion

With all this evidence for the importance of breastfeeding, I leave the final words to Thomas Strong, whose hat says it all. However, the last letter is out of view. The last word on breastfeeding is still a long way into the future.

Postscript

A peak into the future
(tune: 'Jerusalem')

And did those breasts in ancient time
feed every child from birth to five;
and did the nourishment they gave
ensure the human race survived?
And did the nursing night and day
space babies' births by several years,
and did their mothers feed them with joy,
and rarely meet with pain and tears?

Bring back the days when mother's milk
had pride of place at dinner time,
when weaning age was baby-led,
and none was spoon-fed puréed slime.
I will not cease from writing songs
about lactation's mystery
till we've restored our noble breasts
as peaks of human history.

List of illustrations

Cover artwork by Belinda Evans. Email: bagardevans@hotmail.co.uk. Ideas by Alison Blenkinsop (the inspiration for the balloon image came from a child's quote in the book *Fresh Milk* by Fiona Giles, 2003, Simon & Schuster).

Back cover photograph © Michelle Chalmers, by kind permission and courtesy of Anna and Lloyd. *www.michellechalmersphotography.com*

p49   Courtesy of Denise Ives

p53   Courtesy of Anna, Tania and James Lappin

p55   © Heidi Scarfone, by kind permission
www.heidiscarfone.com

p57   Courtesy of Anita, Nikos and Eleni

p62   Courtesy of LC Carol Walton

p67   © Suzanne Colson, by kind permission
www.biologicalnurturing.com

p69   Artwork by Belinda Evans, idea by Alison

p74   © Philippa Pearson-Glaze/La Leche League, by kind permission

p75   © Michelle Chalmers, by kind permission
www.michellechalmersphotography.com

p76   Courtesy of Judith and David, photo by Peter Bradley

p81   Courtesy of Sophia and George

p85   Courtesy of Doris Connor

p87   © Mike Brady, by kind permission
www.babymilkaction.org

p88   © Philippa Pearson-Glaze/La Leche League, by kind permission

p89   © Cassie Pearson

p90   Alarmed image reproduced by kind permission of the Health Promotion Agency for Northern Ireland
www.publichealth.hscni.net

p91   Courtesy of William and Alex Strong

p93   © Posy Simmonds. By kind permission of Posy Simmonds and *The Guardian* newspaper

p94   Artwork by Belinda Evans, idea by Alison

p95   Artwork by Belinda Evans, idea by Alison

ILLUSTRATIONS

Part Two

Contact details

Author
Alison Blenkinsop
Email: aliblenk@hotmail.com
www.linkable.biz

UK agencies and NGOs
Baby Milk Action
34 Trumpington Street, Cambridge, CB2 1QY
01223 464420
www.babymilkaction.org

Baby Feeding Law Group – monitoring the babyfood industry
www.babyfeedinglawgroup.org.uk

Baby Friendly Initiative
020 7312 7652
www.babyfriendly.org.uk

Best Beginnings
020 7443 7895
www.bestbeginnings.org.uk

Boobie Buddies breastfeeding dolls
07976 706838
www.boobiebuddiesbfdolls.co.uk

Breastfeeding Manifesto Coalition
020 8830 5576
www.breastfeedingmanifesto.org.uk

DIPEx charity (Personal Experiences of Health and Illness)
www.healthtalkonline.org

Lactation Consultants of Great Britain
PO Box 56, Virginia Water GU25 4WB
www.lcgb.org

Lact-helpers – Yahoo chat group for breastfeeding supporters
www.groups.yahoo.com

Mama Pack (green alternative to Bounty)
01702 416128
www.mamapacks.eu

UK Association for Milk Banking
0203 313 3559
www.ukamb.org

Voluntary support agencies

National breastfeeding helpline 0300 100 0212

Association of Breastfeeding Mothers
Enquiries: 08444 122948
Counselling helpline: 08444 122 949
www.abm.me.uk

CONTACT DETAILS

Breastfeeding Network
Enquiries: 0844 412 0995
Supporterline: 0300 100 0210
www.breastfeedingnetwork.org.uk

La Leche League
Enquiries: 0845 456 1855
Helpline: 0845 120 2918
www.laleche.org.uk

National Childbirth Trust
Enquiries: 0300 330 0770
Pregnancy and birth helpline: 0300 330 0772
Breastfeeding helpline: 0300 330 0771
www.nct.org.uk

The Baby Café Charitable Trust
www.thebabycafe.org

International agencies: breastfeeding information

Emergency Nutrition Network
www.ennonline.net

United Nations Children's Fund: Infant and Young Child Feeding
www.unicef.org/nutrition/index_breastfeeding

World Alliance for Breastfeeding Action
www.waba.org.my

World Health Organisation: Breastfeeding
www.who.int/topics/breastfeeding

Endnotes

Sources, credits and references

1. *The Politics of Breastfeeding*, third edition, Chapter 21. Gabrielle Palmer (2003), Pinter & Martin

2. Child Poverty Action Group: *Wellbeing and income inequality. www.cpag.org.uk*

3. NHS: The Information Centre. *Infant Feeding Survey 2005. www.ic.nhs.uk/pubs/ifs2005*

4. Baby Milk Action gives regular updates on this topic *www.babymilkaction.org*

5. Quotation by kind permission of Dia L Michels. *Milk, Money & Madness: The Culture and Politics of Breastfeeding.* Naomi Baumslag & Dia Michels (2005), Praeger

6. Reproduced by kind permission of Pam Ayres. *With These Hands*, Pam Ayers (1998), Orion Books

7. Source unknown

8. Reproduced by kind permission of Nigel Rees from *Babes and Sucklings*, Unwin Paperbacks (out of print)

9. The Sabrina (Norma Sykes) site. *www.nylon.net/sabrina*

10. Nell McAndrew official website. *www.nellmcandrew.tv*

11. Reproduced by kind permission of Nigel Rees

12. *What Mothers Do: Especially When It Looks Like Nothing*, Naomi Stadlen (2004), Piatkus

13. For more information and research, visit Doula UK – *www.doula.org.uk*

14. Kangaroo Mother Care. *www.kangaroomothercare.com*

15. Biological Nurturing. *www.biologicalnurturing.com*

16. From 'Womb to World: A Metabolic Perspective', Suzanne Colson (2002). *Midwifery Today* Issue 61. *www.midwiferytoday.com/articles/womb.asp*

17. Child Rearing Practices of Distant Ancestors Foster Morality, Compassion in Kids. *Science Daily* 22 September 2010. *www.sciencedaily.com*

18. Slingmeet gives information about slings and puts baby-wearing mothers in touch with each other. *www.slingmeet.co.uk*

19. One Breast is Enough. *Mothering,* Issue 29 (2005). *www.mothering.com/breastfeeding/one-breast-enough*

20. Lactation Consultants of Great Britain. *www.lcgb.org/shop*

21. a) Government Equalities Office: *Equality Act 2010. www.equalities.gov.uk* & Office of Public Sector Information *www.opsi.gov.uk*
    b) *Breastfeeding etc. (Scotland) Act 2005.* This act states that it is an offence to prevent a child under the age of two years being fed milk in any public place where children are lawfully permitted.

22. Thoughts on Breastfeeding. *www.kathydettwyler.org/dettwyler.html*

23. Child Rearing Practices of Distant Ancestors Foster Morality, Compassion in Kids. *Science Daily* 22 September 2010. *www.sciencedaily.com*

24. *The Churchyard.* S. Mays, C. Harding and C.Heighway (2007), York University Archaeological Publications

25. *Breastfeeding key to saving children's lives.* World Health Organisation (2010) *www.who.int*

26. *Ages and Stages; Babies and Children; Your Toddler.* The Food Standards Agency *www.eatwell.gov.uk*

27. *www.linkable.biz*

28. *Breastfeeding etc. (Scotland) Act 2005.* (See 21b)

29. LAM – the Lactational Amenorrhea Method. World Alliance for Breastfeeding *www.waba.org.my*

30. Ladywell Convent *www.ladywellretreat.org.uk*

31. For more information, visit *www.practicegodspresence.com*

32. *The Scientification of Love.* Michel Odent (2001), Free Association Books, p124. Reproduced by kind permission.

33. Reproduced courtesy of Steve Tomkins. *www.shipoffools.com*

34. This story is found on several internet sites.

35. Paraphrased from *A Treatise on the Miracles of St Francis* by Thomas of Celano, in *The Francis Trilogy of Thomas of Celano.* Eds Armstrong, Hellman and Short (1998). 2005 edition published by New City Press.

Part Two

36. NHS: The Information Centre. *Infant Feeding Survey 2005. www.ic.nhs.uk/pubs/ifs2005*

37. Reverse Pressure Softening information, written by LC Jean Cotterman, is available on several sites via an internet search.

ENDNOTES

38. Search for 'the warm bottle method for expressing breastmilk' on *www.who.int*

39. Correspondence from Professor Dunn can be read on the Archives of Disease in Childhood site under 'Recent eLetters'. Search for 'Tongue-Tie and Infant Feeding.' *www.adc.bmj.com/letters*

40. An abstract of the research can be read on the Wiley Online Library. Search for 'Randomized, controlled trial of division of tongue-tie in infants with feeding problems'. *www.onlinelibrary.wiley.com*

41. Lactation Consultants of Great Britain. *www.lcgb.org/shop*

42. Brian Palmer's website is *www.brianpalmerdds.com*

43. 'Breast-milk: The White Blood'. *www.borntolove.com*

44. *The Politics of Breastfeeding*, p56.

45. Attachment parenting is described on various internet sites, and is the subject of a book by William and Martha Sears.

46. A CNN film can be found on YouTube under 'Miracle Baby's Life Revived by Mother's Touch'.

47. Source unknown.

48. 'A short history' text reproduced with permission from the Photo Gallery of the Kangaroo Mother Care website. Joan Norton is Jill Bergman's mother. *www.kangaroomothercare.com*

49. UK Baby Friendly Initiative. *www.babyfriendly.org.uk* (The organisation made no contribution to the song)

50. International Board of Lactation Consultants Examiners. *www.iblce.org*

51. Search for 'woolly breasts appeal goes global'. *www.bbc.co.uk*

52. Search for 'knitted breasts help new mothers'. *www.bbc.co.uk*

53. *Midwifery Best Practice* Vol 2. Ed Sara Wickham (2004), Elsevier. *www.elsevier.com*

54. 'What's in a nappy?' leaflet from National Childbirth Trust, *www.nctsales.co.uk*

55. *www.knittinginmybackyarn.blogspot.com*

56. Source unknown.

57. Search for 'Spanish piglet suckled by her canine carer'. *www.bbc.co.uk*

58. Reproduced by kind permission from *Breastfeeding at a Glance: Facts, Figures and Trivia about Lactation* by Dia Michels & Cynthia Good Mojab, with Naomi Bromberg Bar-Yam. *www.platypusmedia.com*

59. Extract from *There is a smart drug – it's called breast milk* by Johann Hari. *The Independent*, 19 June 2008.

60. 'Breastfeeding saves mothers' lives: lactation consultant Alison Blenkinsop discusses how breastfeeding affects maternal mortality in the developing world.' *www.thefreelibrary.com*

61. *What the Dog Saw*, p101. Malcolm Gladwell (2009), Penguin.

62. 'Breast cancer: What is breast cancer?' Article was reviewed in June 2009. *www.netdoctor.co.uk*

63. One Million Campaign. *www.onemillioncampaign.org*

64. Deliver Now for Women and Children. *www.delivernow.org*. The film can be seen on YouTube; search for 'Deliver Now for Women and Children – Breastfeeding (colostrum)'.

65. Information courtesy of Professor Dunn.

66. Formula guidance. *www.babymilkaction.org*

67. Midwifery Training Grants. Search for 'Danone'. *www.tommys.org*

68. 'Midwives should tell Danone to keep its ill-gotten Aptamil loot'. *www.babymilkaction.org*

69. Search for 'danger sore boobs'. *www.babymilkaction.org*

70. Reproduced courtesy of the Food Commission *www.foodmagazine.org.uk*

71. Search for 'NHS Choices Blenkinsop'. *www.nhs.uk*

72. *www.petitiononline.com/dbm*

73. 'More Ways to Use Breastmilk.' Reproduced by kind permission from an article in the Nov/Dec 2005 issue of *Mothering* magazine. *www.mothering.com*

74. 'Substance in Breast Milk Kills Cancer Cells, Study Suggests.' *Science Daily*, 23 April 2010. *www.sciencedaily.com*

Also available from Lonely Scribe

HOME BIRTHS
stories to inspire and inform

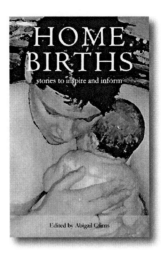

A moving collection of real life stories celebrating the joy and wonder of birth at home. This collection of first-hand recollections by mothers and their partners gives an insight into the modern experience of home birth, from the first decision to the final push.

"The pushing stage involved me on all fours grunting and sipping cups of tea between pushes. One of the midwives joked that it was the most sedate second stage she had ever seen. Fred was born in the corner of our bedroom."

"Two hours after the birth we were were left alone at home: the three of us, a bottle of bubbly and the cat."

ISBN 978-1-905179-02-2 • £13.99/$24.99

ORDER FORM

Please send me ____ copies of *Home Births* at a cost of £12 each (RRP £13.99) plus £3 total postage per order.

☐ I enclose a cheque for £ _____

Name: _____

Address: _____

_____

_____

Telephone: _____

Email: _____

Return to: Lonely Scribe, Welwyn, Bermuda Avenue,
Little Eaton, Derbyshire DE21 5DG

Lightning Source UK Ltd.
Milton Keynes UK
UKOW04f1439190915

258863UK00002B/30/P